Published by **Saklas Publishing**
ISBN: 979-8-9943016-0-9

Disclaimer

This work is an independent scholarly and interpretive analysis. It is not affiliated with, endorsed by, or representative of Anton Szandor *Lavey*, the Church of Satan, or any associated organization. All trademarks, names, and titles referenced are used solely for purposes of analysis, commentary, and critique.

This book does not provide religious instruction, occult guidance, or spiritual counseling. It examines belief systems, rituals, and symbolic frameworks as cultural and psychological phenomena. Nothing in this work should be construed as an endorsement of any ideology, practice, or organization discussed herein.

First Edition

The Satanic Bible:
Consciousness Technology
Rupture, Identity, and the
Architecture of Enclosure

-A Prison Interview-

Frater Lachesis Peyton

Table of Contents

BOOK ONE v

   INTRODUCTION 1

      Chapter One: 8

      Chapter Two: 12

      Chapter Three 17

      Chapter Four 21

      Chapter Five 25

      Chapter Six 29

      Chapter Seven 34

   CONCLUSION 40

BOOK TWO 50

      Chapter One 51

      Chapter Two 57

      Chapter Three 63

      Chapter Four 69

      Chapter Five 75

      Chapter Six 80

      Chapter Seven 84

BOOK THREE 88

   Introduction – A Lens, Not a System 90

   The Seven Elyalithic Axioms 91

   Closure 117

   BOOK ONE – REFERENCES 118

BOOK TWO – REFERENCES...120

BOOK THREE – REFERENCES...123

BOOK ONE

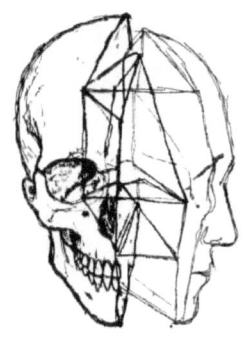

INTRODUCTION

Method, Sources, and the Architecture of a Diagnostic Monograph

This book is a diagnostic and interpretive monograph. It treats Anton Szandor Lavey's *The Satanic Bible* not primarily as theology to be affirmed or refuted, but as a functional system designed to produce specific psychological and social effects. The analysis focuses on how the text operates as what may be described, analytically, as a form of consciousness technology: a structured set of rhetorical, symbolic, and ritual procedures that reorganize belief, identity, and will through deliberate mechanisms rather than supernatural claims.

Methodologically, this approach aligns with established practices in the academic study of religion that emphasize close reading combined with theoretical lenses rather than exhaustive exegesis. Stausberg and Engler describe such synthetic diagnostic monographs as a standard scholarly mode for analyzing how religious texts function structurally and experientially, particularly when the goal is to map mechanisms rather than to catalogue doctrines (Stausberg & Engler, 2011). In this tradition, interpretation proceeds through structural mapping, comparative framing, and attention to effects in lived experience rather than line-by-line commentary.

Psychologists of religion similarly note that analytic work may legitimately foreground what a system does to cognition, emotion, and identity, provided that interpretations are grounded in close engagement with the primary text and articulated through explicit conceptual frameworks (Streib & Hood, 2013). This book follows that model. When it summarizes Laveyan ideas in compressed or aphoristic form, the intent is not to reproduce original phrasing, but to state the operational logic of the system in plain terms. Readers seeking verbatim language are directed to *The Satanic Bible* itself.

Consciousness Technology, Rupture, and Enclosure

The concept of consciousness technology is not unique to Laveyan Satanism. Scholars of modern esotericism and popular religion have long observed that many late-modern spiritual and ideological systems present themselves as tools for liberation from inherited guilt, repression, or constraint, promising freedom through deliberate operations on belief and identity (Hanegraaff, 1996). These systems often succeed at producing powerful subjective effects—clarity, vitality, relief—while simultaneously installing new, subtler forms of enclosure.

Carrette and King describe this dynamic in contemporary self-help and corporate spirituality, where practices marketed as emancipatory frequently normalize new regimes of self-monitoring and productivity, transforming tools of liberation into what they call "elegant cages" (Carrette & King, 2005).

Similar patterns have been documented in therapeutic contexts, where techniques designed to enhance awareness or autonomy can produce both relief and distress depending on dosage, context, and the practitioner's capacity for integration (Farias & Wikholm, 2015).

This book argues that *The Satanic Bible* represents a particularly clear instance of this broader phenomenon. Lavey's system is unusually explicit about its rejection of transcendence, its emphasis on self-interest, and its use of ritual as psychodrama rather than supernatural invocation. Precisely because of this clarity, it provides a valuable case study for understanding how consciousness technologies function when stripped of metaphysical ambiguity.

New Religious Movements, Self-Religion, and Identity Construction

The analytical framing employed here draws extensively on scholarship in the study of new religious movements (NRMs) and self-religion. Barker's classic work on the Unification Church demonstrated that conversion to new movements often involves narratives of liberation from prior enclosures alongside the cultivation of highly structured identities that can later feel constraining from the inside (Barker, 1984). Beckford similarly emphasized that NRMs operate as laboratories for intense identity work, balancing promises of autonomy with organizational techniques that stabilize belonging through boundary reinforcement and oppositional posture (Beckford, 1985).

Subsequent scholarship has extended these insights to post-traditional and highly individualized spiritual systems. Arweck and Clarke note that many fringe or alternative movements blend therapeutic, political, and spiritual discourses into comprehensive "technologies of the self," shaping how adherents experience freedom and constraint simultaneously (Arweck & Clarke, 1997). De Keere further argues that late-modern individuals are encouraged to pursue personal growth through individualized spiritual paths that sacralize freedom while quietly prescribing narrow repertoires of acceptable feeling and conduct (De Keere, 2025).

Laveyan Satanism fits squarely within this landscape. Laycock characterizes it as an atheistic self-religion in which Satanic symbolism functions as a narrative device for constructing the self as lucid rebel, with group belonging organized around shared refusal rather than shared belief (Laycock, 2015). This book adopts that framing while extending it to examine not only how such identity construction empowers practitioners, but how it can also limit later development.

Rupture, Development, and the Problem of Integration

A central claim of this book is that Lavey's system succeeds brilliantly at rupture while failing catastrophically at integration. This claim is not moralistic; it is developmental. Erikson's theory of identity formation provides a useful baseline. Erikson describes periods of ideological experimentation and confrontation with authority as necessary for ego consolidation, particularly in adolescence and early adulthood (Erikson, 1968). Rupture, in this sense, is not pathology but phase.

4

Problems arise when rupture hardens into foreclosure: the premature fixation of identity around a single stance that resists revision. Research on former members of world-rejecting movements supports this trajectory. Black's qualitative study documents how such groups often function as temporary solutions to crises of autonomy and belonging, with later exits driven by the need to integrate autonomy with relational connection (Black, 2011).

The pattern recurs across domains. Houtman and Aupers show that post-traditional spiritualities prioritize individual choice and inner experience while installing new internalized norms that structure autonomy and authenticity (Houtman & Aupers, 2007). In mental-health research, studies of Satanist identity indicate that while identification can buffer against depressive symptoms under certain conditions, it also correlates with anticipated stigma and ongoing tension around meaning and morality (Sprankle et al., 2019; Minnesota State University, 2022).

The New Iron Cage

Critical social theory provides additional language for describing this dynamic. Horkheimer and Adorno argued that projects of rational self-mastery aimed at emancipation can solidify into new forms of domination when controlling logics are internalized and experienced as freedom (Horkheimer & Adorno, 2002). Ritzer's reformulation of Weber's "iron cage" thesis shows how rationalized systems promise efficiency and control while producing environments of constraint that practitioners both rely on and feel trapped within (Ritzer, 1993).

Bauman's analysis of liquid modernity further clarifies why such systems are appealing. In a social world characterized by fragility and constant renegotiation, highly articulated identity frameworks offer stability, even as they demand continuous maintenance (Bauman, 2000). Laveyan Satanism, with its emphasis on self-authorship and disciplined rebellion, can be read as both a response to and a symptom of these conditions.

Vedantic Guna Theory as Diagnostic Lens

To illuminate the internal dynamics of Lavey's system, this book employs Vedantic guna theory as a diagnostic lens, not as doctrine or influence claim. Classical Vedantic philosophy describes sattva, rajas, and tamas as dynamic qualities of mind and matter whose relative predominance shapes clarity, agitation, and inertia (Puligandla, 1975). Contemporary psychological research has operationalized these concepts, finding reliable correlations between guna profiles and measures of stress, life satisfaction, and well-being (Wolf, 1999; Krishnan, 2022).

These findings support the use of guna theory as an interpretive model for analyzing modern texts. When applied to *The Satanic Bible*, the pattern becomes clear. The system is heavily rajasic and tamasic: it emphasizes action, drive, and opposition while rejecting rest, permeability, and receptive clarity. Sattva—the capacity for clarity without reactivity and integration without collapse—is conspicuously absent. The consequence is predictable: short-term empowerment followed by chronic arousal, relational thinning, and exhaustion.

Scope, Limits, and Audience

This book does not offer a redemptive synthesis or a prescriptive path forward. Doing so would repeat the error it critiques. Instead, it provides criteria for recognizing when rupture has completed its work and when integration becomes necessary. These criteria are offered as tools, not commandments. Their application remains the reader's responsibility.

Book One is diagnostic. Readers need not agree with the critique; they need only follow the analysis. Book Two provides tools rather than doctrine, to be used selectively and discarded when no longer useful. Throughout, the emphasis remains on mechanisms and effects rather than on belief.

The intended audience includes scholars of new religious movements, practitioners or former practitioners of Laveyan and adjacent systems, and general readers interested in how belief systems function as technologies of identity. Across these audiences, the central question remains the same: not whether *The Satanic Bible* works, but what its work ultimately produces.

Chapter One:

Historical and Intellectual Context

Anton Szandor Lavey, born Howard Stanton Levey on April 11, 1930, in Chicago, Illinois, emerged in the latter half of the twentieth century as the most visible figure associated with modern Satanism. Scholarly treatments consistently describe his early life as relatively conventional, offering little evidence for the dramatic origins and formative encounters later attributed to him in autobiographical and movement-produced narratives. Academic historians therefore treat Lavey's biography with particular caution, emphasizing the gap between verifiable documentation and the persona he would later cultivate as founder and high priest of the Church of Satan (Lewis, 2001; Introvigne, 2016).

Lavey spent most of his youth in California and did not complete formal secondary education. He attended Tamalpais High School in Mill Valley but left before graduation, and no independent records substantiate later claims of college-level study in criminology or related disciplines. Rather than interpreting this trajectory as an early ideological rejection of institutional learning, scholars generally frame it as a pragmatic disengagement that preceded a turn toward informal, performance-based labor. Lavey's later hostility toward academic, clerical, and bureaucratic authority appears in this reading as a retrospective philosophical stance rather than a motivating cause (Lewis, 2001).

Music represents the most reliably documented aspect of Lavey's early adult life. He earned modest income as a nightclub organist during the late 1940s and 1950s, establishing a livelihood within local entertainment circuits. While Lavey later embellished this period with claims of circus employment, burlesque orchestras, and prestigious engagements, academic studies note the absence of corroborating archival evidence and treat such stories as part of a broader pattern of narrative inflation. Scholars emphasize that these embellishments functioned symbolically, elevating ordinary entertainment work into mythic apprenticeship narratives consistent with charismatic self-presentation (Dyrendal, Lewis, & Petersen, 2015).

Claims that Lavey worked as a photographer for the San Francisco Police Department during the early 1950s occupy a similar status in the literature. Although Lavey repeatedly invoked this alleged experience to ground his pessimistic view of human nature, independent verification has not been established, and academic accounts consistently frame the story as uncorroborated. Rather than adjudicating the claim on evidentiary grounds alone, scholars analyze its rhetorical function, noting how narratives of proximity to violence and institutional brutality serve to legitimize moral conclusions presented as empirically derived rather than ideologically chosen (Lewis, 2012; Dyrendal et al., 2015).

By the late 1950s, Lavey's personal relationships and domestic arrangements became increasingly intertwined with his emerging public activities. He married Carole Lansing in the early 1950s, with whom he had a daughter, Karla Lavey, before the marriage ended in divorce. He later entered a long-term partnership with Diane Hegarty, who played a significant administrative and organizational role in his later endeavors. Authorized biographical accounts emphasize Hegarty's responsibility for correspondence, scheduling, and internal logistics, while independent scholars stress the infrastructural rather than ideological significance of this partnership (Barton, 1990; Lewis, 2001).

During the early 1960s, Lavey hosted a series of informal lectures and gatherings in San Francisco that later came to be remembered as the "Magic Circle." Academic treatments describe these meetings not as a coherent religious body but as a salon combining sensational lectures, occult themes, and theatrical provocation. The gatherings provided a space in which Lavey could test rhetorical strategies, symbolic inversions, and audience responses before committing them to fixed doctrine. This experimental phase is widely understood as a precursor to institutionalization rather than as an already formed religious movement (Introvigne, 2016; Lewis, 2001).

The public declaration of the Church of Satan in 1966 is consistently interpreted by scholars as a calculated act of symbolic inversion rather than the emergence of a new supernatural belief system. The choice of Walpurgisnacht as a founding date and the adoption of Satanic imagery functioned as deliberate provocations aimed at a media-saturated countercultural environment. Sociological analyses characterize Laveyan Satanism as a form of secular or symbolic religion, in which Satan operates as an emblem of individualism, pride, and resistance to Christian moral authority rather than as a literal metaphysical entity (Petersen, 2008; Laycock, 2015).

Within this framework, ritual occupies a central but carefully circumscribed role. Lavey explicitly rejected belief in supernatural forces, framing ritual instead as symbolic psychodrama designed to channel emotion, reinforce ego boundaries, and provide controlled catharsis. Scholars situate this approach within broader twentieth-century currents of self-religion and identity construction, in which religious forms are retained while transcendental claims are abandoned (Petersen, 2008).

The publication of *The Satanic Bible* in 1969 marked the consolidation of ideas previously rehearsed in performance, lecture, and media interaction. Academic analyses emphasize that the text functions as a constructed synthesis rather than a revealed scripture, combining selective borrowings from earlier thinkers with contemporary countercultural rhetoric. Studies have documented Lavey's unacknowledged reliance on Ragnar Redbeard's *Might Is Right*, parallels with Ayn Rand's ethical egoism, simplified appropriations of Nietzschean critique, and ritual aesthetics drawn from Crowleyan ceremonial magic. These elements are understood not as systematic philosophical engagement but as instrumental adaptations assembled for rhetorical force and symbolic clarity (Dyrendal et al., 2015; Introvigne, 2016).

Sociologically, Laveyan Satanism is commonly classified as a form of identity-based or self-religion, centered on charismatic authority and symbolic deviance. Scholars note that Lavey's carefully managed image and narrative control were essential to maintaining cohesion and distinction during the movement's early years, while the same emphasis on individualism contributed to later fragmentation once personal authority diminished (Lewis, 2012; Laycock, 2015).

Viewed in historical context, Lavey's significance lies less in the factual accuracy of his autobiographical claims than in his ability to transform biography itself into an ideological tool. His life narrative operates as a mechanism of rupture, destabilizing inherited moral frameworks and inviting adherents to reconceive identity as performative and self-authored. The chapters that follow examine this machinery at the level of doctrine, ritual, and psychological effect.

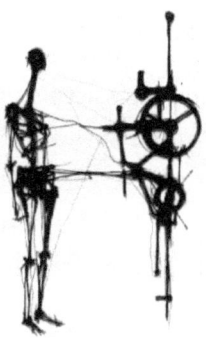

Chapter Two:

The Nine Satanic Statements and Core Philosophy

The Nine Satanic Statements appear as a standalone doctrinal block near the front of Anton Szandor Lavey's *The Satanic Bible* and function as the system's threshold text (Lavey, 1969, p. 13). They are presented in a compact, numbered sequence with no preliminary explanation, and that placement is itself part of their psychological operation. This chapter treats the statements as consciousness technology, meaning a set of linguistic devices designed to install new permissions, new boundaries, and a new self-conception. The analysis that follows distinguishes between Lavey's quoted doctrine and the interpretive claims made here, and it marks that distinction through explicit attribution and page-specific citation.

Lavey's decision to lead with these statements is not a neutral editorial choice. He does not invite the reader into a discussion but initiates the reader into a posture. The statements function as reversals, and reversals work most efficiently when delivered as declarations rather than as arguments. The result is an immediate cognitive pivot, where inherited moral reflexes are forced into confrontation.

The statements also serve as identity technology, because they define the practitioner through what is refused and what is claimed. The language is binary, and the binaries are moralized through inversion, with Christian virtues reclassified as weakness and Satanic virtues framed as realism. This produces cohesion through opposition, because shared refusal becomes a shared bond. It also produces risk, because identity anchored in opposition must continually locate an enemy to remain coherent.

The first statement reads, "Satan represents indulgence, instead of abstinence!" (Lavey, 1969, p. 13). The sentence is structurally simple, but its psychological function is complex because it grants permission while naming its enemy. Indulgence is positioned as corrective rather than as excess, and abstinence is framed as imposed deprivation rather than as discipline. The operational effect is the dismantling of guilt, particularly in readers conditioned to equate desire with moral failure.

When this permission lands, it often produces a felt shift before it produces an articulated belief. The reader is licensed to stop negotiating with internal prohibitions and to treat desire as natural rather than corrupt. In practice, this can restore agency to people whose lives have been organized around denial. The failure mode appears when the permission is treated as an end state rather than as a phase, because indulgence without discernment can become compulsion by another name.

The second statement reads, "Satan represents vital existence, instead of spiritual pipe dreams!" (Lavey, 1969, p. 13). Here Lavey installs a metaphysical boundary by defining the real as bodily and immediate and defining the transcendent as evasive fantasy. The phrase "vital existence" carries a biological authority, while "pipe dreams" frames spiritual aspiration as childish self-deception. The operational effect is grounding, and it pulls attention from imagined salvation toward concrete life.

13

For readers prone to dissociation, this statement can feel like a return of weight and traction. It pushes the practitioner toward responsibility for the conditions of life, including health, work, conflict, and desire. It also hardens the system's suspicion of permeability, because any openness to transcendence is pre-coded as weakness or escape. Over time, the same grounding that builds potency can flatten the psyche if it eliminates wonder, renewal, or symbolic depth.

The third statement reads, "Satan represents undefiled wisdom, instead of hypocritical self-deceit!" (Lavey, 1969, p. 13). The key term here is "undefiled," which frames wisdom as something contaminated by social piety and purified by ruthless clarity. Lavey targets the gap between professed virtue and enacted appetite, and he defines that gap as hypocrisy. The operational effect is a mandate for exposure, first of institutions and then of the self.

This statement can cultivate discernment when it is applied inward with equal rigor. It trains the practitioner to identify self-flattering rationalizations and to replace them with a harsher, more coherent self-account. The failure mode emerges when "undefiled wisdom" becomes a performance of brutality, used to wound others while shielding the practitioner's own contradictions. In that form, the statement becomes a tool of selective blindness, not clarity.

The fourth statement reads, "Satan represents kindness to those who deserve it, instead of love wasted on ingrates!" (Lavey, 1969, p. 13). Lavey replaces unconditional love with conditional allocation and frames indiscriminate compassion as waste. The language of "deserve" installs judgment as virtue, and the language of "wasted" turns emotional care into an economic resource to be guarded. The operational effect is boundary enforcement, particularly for those trained into compulsive caretaking.

In many cases, this statement enables people to exit exploitative relational patterns without guilt. It legitimizes refusal and reclassifies self-preservation as ethical rather than selfish. The failure mode occurs when the practitioner's criteria for "deserving" narrow into distrust, and then distrust becomes identity. In that condition, kindness becomes a rationed currency and intimacy becomes structurally difficult.

The fifth statement reads, "Satan represents vengeance, instead of turning the other cheek!" (Lavey, 1969, p. 13). This is the most explicit reversal of Christian restraint, and it installs retaliation as moral clarity. Psychologically, it releases suppressed anger and legitimizes the impulse to strike back. The operational effect is empowerment through aggression, particularly in people trained to collapse under harm.

At its best, the statement can support decisive boundary enforcement and the termination of abusive dynamics. At its worst, it can turn grievance into a permanent engine, keeping the practitioner locked in cycles of replay and escalation. Vengeance sustains opposition, and opposition sustains the identity the system is building. That is precisely why the statement works and precisely why it can later enclose.

The sixth statement reads, "Satan represents responsibility to the responsible, instead of concern for psychic vampires!" (Lavey, 1969, p. 13). Here the system defines certain relational demands as parasitic and frames withdrawal as sanity. The phrase "psychic vampires" provides a vivid label that collapses nuance into a single category of threat. The operational effect is the reduction of guilt-based obligation and the reallocation of energy toward reciprocal bonds.

This statement can be genuinely corrective for people trapped in codependent patterns. It trains the practitioner to discriminate between reciprocity and extraction, and it grants moral permission to say no. The failure mode appears when the vampire category becomes overly expansive and is used to justify indifference toward ordinary human

15

need. In that form, the statement becomes a solvent that dissolves empathy rather than a tool that repairs boundaries.

The seventh statement reads, "Satan represents man as just another animal, sometimes better, more often worse than those that walk on all fours" (Lavey, 1969, p. 13). This statement grounds the system in carnal reality by rejecting claims of spiritual superiority. Human animal nature is accepted without shame rather than denied through moral abstraction. Embodiment deepens under this framing, though it carries the risk of reducing human behavior to predation mechanics when applied without integration.

The eighth statement reads, "Satan represents all of the so-called sins, as they all lead to physical, mental, or emotional gratification" (Lavey, 1969, p. 13). This statement reframes taboos as natural fulfillments rather than moral failures. Permission is extended to pleasure as a legitimate source of vitality rather than corruption. The psychological effect integrates previously repressed drives, stabilizing density and desire when held in balance rather than excess.

The ninth statement reads, "Satan has been the best friend the Church has ever had, as He has kept it in business all these years" (Lavey, 1969, p. 13). This final declaration functions as an ironic capstone that exposes how opposition sustains the systems it claims to resist. Christianity's reliance on the Devil for definitional clarity is rendered explicit rather than concealed. The statement reveals how belief systems maintain cohesion through transgression and shared antagonism.

In plain terms, the Nine Satanic Statements deliver shock therapy for those emerging from guilt-based morality. They grant permission, ground awareness, sharpen discernment, conserve energy, and prioritize the self. For individuals trapped in pathological self-denial, these effects can be genuinely emancipatory. The problem arises when initial liberation hardens into a perpetual defensive posture that no longer serves growth

Chapter Three

The Book of Satan – Rupture as Shock Technology

The Book of Satan occupies a distinct and aggressive position within *The Satanic Bible*. It is not an instructional manual, nor a metaphysical treatise, nor a ritual guide. Its primary function is rupture. The section is designed to break inherited moral architectures through sustained rhetorical assault, replacing guilt-based restraint with antagonistic self-assertion. This chapter analyzes the Book of Satan as shock technology: a deliberately destabilizing apparatus engineered to fracture internalized authority structures through inversion, provocation, and contempt.

Scholars of Laveyan Satanism have repeatedly noted that the Book of Satan differs qualitatively from the rest of *The Satanic Bible*. While later sections discuss ethics, ritual, and practice in relatively measured terms, the Book of Satan operates almost exclusively through polemic (Dyrendal, Lewis, & Petersen, 2015). Its tone is bombastic, absolutist, and intentionally abrasive. The text does not invite dialogue or gradual persuasion; it declares war on what it frames as hypocrisy, weakness, and moral deception.

This stylistic excess is not accidental. The language of the Book of Satan closely mirrors the rhetoric of Ragnar Redbeard's *Might Is Right*, from which substantial portions are adapted with minimal modification (Redbeard, 1896; Dyrendal et al., 2015). In Lavey's recontextualization, overtly racist and biologically supremacist material is largely excised, but the core Social Darwinist contempt for weakness, egalitarianism, and altruism remains intact. The text also adopts a deliberately archaic, scriptural cadence. Sentences are short, declarative, and rhythmically reminiscent of biblical prose. By borrowing the sonic authority of scripture while reversing its moral content, the Book of Satan exploits familiarity to generate cognitive dissonance. The reader recognizes the form of moral law even as its substance is violently inverted, a technique scholars have described as parody functioning less as humor than as weaponized inversion (Dyrendal et al., 2015).

From a psychological perspective, such inversion operates as shock. Sudden moral reversals disrupt habitual patterns of evaluation, particularly in readers whose identities have been shaped by rigid religious or moral systems. Erikson's theory of identity development provides a useful lens here. Erikson describes ideological confrontation with authority as a normal component of identity consolidation during periods of crisis or transition (Erikson, 1968). The Book of Satan accelerates this process by collapsing nuance and forcing confrontation. There is no gradual renegotiation of values; there is only rejection.

Importantly, this rupture does not depend on belief in a literal Satan. Lavey explicitly rejected supernaturalism, framing Satan as a symbolic construct rather than a metaphysical being (Lavey, 1969). Within this framework, the Book of Satan functions as psychodrama: an enacted rebellion in which defiance is rehearsed internally and identity is reorganized around refusal.

This performance has measurable psychological effects. Laycock argues that Laveyan Satanism constructs the self through oppositional narrative, with coherence achieved by shared refusal rather than shared belief (Laycock, 2015). The Book of Satan provides the raw material for that narrative. It supplies a vocabulary of contempt and strength that allows practitioners to reinterpret prior experiences of subordination as evidence of moral clarity rather than failure.

The difficulty arises when rupture is treated as an endpoint rather than as a transitional phase. Developmental and sociological studies of world-rejecting movements consistently show that radical breaks from prior identity structures can stabilize the self temporarily while creating long-term constraints when revision is discouraged (Black, 2011). The Book of Satan offers no mechanism for reassessment. It does not distinguish between necessary rupture and permanent antagonism. Instead, it presents opposition as a stable and desirable posture.

This has predictable consequences. When identity coherence depends on opposition, antagonism must be continually renewed. The subject learns to experience equilibrium as weakness and reconciliation as capitulation. Anger ceases to function as a situational signal and becomes a standing orientation. The Book of Satan provides no criteria for knowing when rupture has completed its work. Without such criteria, the practitioner risks remaining in a perpetual state of defensive arousal.

Scholars have noted that Lavey's system consistently privileges strength defined as resistance, refusal, and dominance, while offering little language for integration or permeability (Dyrendal et al., 2015; Laycock, 2015). This asymmetry is already visible in the Book of Satan. Compassion is framed as deception, humility as fraud, and restraint as self-betrayal. The possibility that strength might coexist with openness or responsiveness is not explored. Such qualities are preemptively coded as weakness.

The Book of Satan is therefore best understood not as a philosophy of life, but as an intervention. It is a demolition charge placed against internalized authority. Used selectively, it can dismantle pathological obedience and restore agency. Used indiscriminately, it calcifies into a brittle identity that resists growth as fiercely as it once resisted domination.

This interpretation does not dismiss the efficacy of rupture. On the contrary, it takes rupture seriously as a psychological operation. Many practitioners report that the Book of Satan accomplished in weeks what years of therapy had failed to achieve: the dissolution of shame, the legitimization of anger, and the recovery of self-trust (Laycock, 2015). The problem is not that rupture works. The problem is that the text offers no map beyond it.

By presenting rupture as wisdom rather than as phase, the Book of Satan quietly forecloses the possibility of maturation. The reader is trained to identify with the break itself, mistaking intensity for insight and hardness for clarity. In doing so, the system reproduces the very rigidity it claims to oppose.

This chapter does not condemn the Book of Satan. It situates it. Rupture is a necessary operation under specific conditions: when inherited moral systems enforce chronic self-negation, silence anger, or demand submission at the cost of psychological integrity. In such contexts, the Book of Satan functions as an effective shock. What it does not do—and cannot do without undermining its own logic—is teach how to live after the break.

That omission is structural, not accidental. It sets the stage for the techniques of control explored in the Book of Lucifer and for the deeper enclosure that emerges when rupture hardens into identity. Understanding the Book of Satan as shock technology rather than as terminal philosophy is therefore essential for understanding both the power and the limits of Laveyan Satanism.

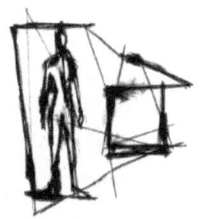

Chapter Four

The Book of Lucifer — Lesser Magic as Social Engineering

The Book of Lucifer shifts the operational center of *The Satanic Bible* from rupture to application. Where the Book of Satan functions as shock technology, the Book of Lucifer introduces what Lavey terms "lesser magic": a set of techniques concerned with influence, manipulation, and social leverage. This section does not seek to overthrow inherited moral authority through attack, but to exploit existing social dynamics once authority has been psychologically dismantled. Its domain is not metaphysical speculation but interpersonal power.

Unlike the polemical aggression of the Book of Satan, the tone of the Book of Lucifer is pragmatic and instructional. Essays address charm, deception, sexual strategy, image management, and the exploitation of human weakness. Lavey presents these techniques as naturalistic extensions of animal behavior, stripped of moral sentimentality. Influence is treated as a skill, not a transgression. The practitioner is encouraged to observe others unsparingly and to use that observation strategically.

Scholars consistently note that lesser magic is the most explicitly psychological component of Laveyan Satanism (Petersen, 2008; Dyrendal et al., 2015). Lavey draws on carnival showmanship, advertising logic, and folk psychology rather than occult metaphysics. The goal is not transformation of reality through ritual, but the rearrangement of probabilities through perception management. Success depends on understanding how desire, fear, and projection operate in everyday social environments.

This reframing can be immediately empowering. For individuals emerging from guilt-based moral systems or chronic social passivity, the Book of Lucifer provides language and tactics for reclaiming agency. Manipulation is no longer shameful; it is reframed as competence. Social interaction becomes legible rather than mystifying. Many practitioners report rapid improvements in confidence, boundary enforcement, and situational control when first applying these principles (Laycock, 2015).

However, the logic of lesser magic carries an inherent risk. Because it treats all social interaction as strategic terrain, it encourages a stance of perpetual calculation. Relationships are evaluated primarily in terms of utility, leverage, and return on investment. Over time, this instrumentalization can erode spontaneity and mutuality. What begins as situational awareness risks becoming a fixed posture.

Laycock characterizes this pattern as the consolidation of oppositional selfhood into managerial identity (Laycock, 2015). The practitioner no longer defines the self merely against external authority, but against vulnerability itself. Emotional openness becomes a liability; trust is reframed as naïveté. The techniques that once protected against exploitation begin to preclude intimacy.

Sociological analyses of self-religions and individualist spiritualities show a similar trajectory. Systems that emphasize autonomy through control often struggle to accommodate relational interdependence without framing it as weakness (Heelas, 1996; Dyrendal et al., 2015). The Book of Lucifer offers no corrective to this tendency. It provides no criteria for when strategic engagement should yield to non-instrumental connection.

This absence is structural rather than accidental. Lesser magic presumes a world of competitors rather than collaborators. Influence is always directional; vulnerability is asymmetrical. While this model may be adaptive in hostile or exploitative environments, it becomes constraining when generalized. The practitioner learns to perform rather than to encounter, to manage impressions rather than to be affected by them.

The result is a subtle enclosure. Social mastery increases while emotional range narrows. The subject may appear more powerful, more controlled, and more effective, yet increasingly isolated. Because the system frames this outcome as strength, the costs often remain unrecognized. Exhaustion, relational thinning, and chronic vigilance are interpreted as the price of sovereignty rather than as warning signs.

The Book of Lucifer thus extends the rupture initiated by the Book of Satan into everyday life. It teaches how to live *after* moral authority has been rejected, but only within the logic of dominance and defense. What it does not teach is how to recognize when those strategies have outlived their usefulness. There is no language for relinquishing control without surrender, or for engaging others without calculation.

This does not negate the efficacy of lesser magic. As a transitional skill set, it can be invaluable. For individuals previously trapped in passivity, manipulation awareness restores agency and self-trust. The problem arises when tactics become identity. When every interaction is treated as

23

contest, the self becomes permanently mobilized, unable to rest or revise.

Understanding the Book of Lucifer as applied rupture clarifies its role within Laveyan Satanism. It operationalizes the break from submission, translating ideological defiance into behavioral competence. Yet by extending antagonism into the social field without limit, it deepens the enclosure initiated by permanent opposition. The practitioner becomes sovereign, but increasingly alone.

This chapter does not moralize manipulation nor romanticize vulnerability. It situates lesser magic developmentally. Used selectively, it protects against exploitation and restores autonomy. Used indiscriminately, it installs a mode of relating that forecloses integration. The same skills that prevent domination can, when absolutized, prevent connection.

The Book of Lucifer therefore marks a critical inflection point in the system. It reveals how rupture hardens into lifestyle, and how liberation begins to resemble enclosure once control becomes continuous. Recognizing this transition is essential for understanding why Laveyan Satanism stabilizes power while quietly eroding relational capacity.

Chapter Five

The Book of Belial — Mastery of Earthly Reality

The Book of Belial marks a decisive shift in *The Satanic Bible* from social manipulation to ritualized will. Where the Book of Lucifer focuses on influence within existing social structures, the Book of Belial introduces what Lavey terms "greater magic": formalized ritual designed to effect change through concentrated emotional and psychological intensity. This section frames magic not as supernatural intervention but as a disciplined technology for directing intent toward material outcomes.

Lavey defines magic as change in accordance with will, explicitly rejecting metaphysical explanations in favor of pragmatic results (Lavey, 1969). Ritual is presented as a means of isolating, amplifying, and discharging emotional energy in a controlled environment. The ritual chamber, tools, and ceremonial sequence function to narrow attention, heighten affect, and suspend ordinary cognitive constraints. The aim is not communion with external forces but internal realignment.

Scholars consistently note that this formulation aligns with secular models of psychodrama and emotional catharsis rather than occult metaphysics (Petersen, 2008; Dyrendal et al., 2015). The efficacy of ritual derives from its capacity to reorganize motivation, perception, and behavior through intensified symbolic enactment. In this sense, greater magic operates as an applied psychology of will.

For many practitioners, this framework proves effective. Ritual provides a sanctioned outlet for emotions that have been morally suppressed—anger, desire, grief—allowing them to be mobilized rather than repressed. Participants often report increased clarity, decisiveness, and a sense of regained agency following ritual performance (Laycock, 2015). As with rupture and lesser magic, the immediate effects can be dramatic.

However, the structure of greater magic carries a familiar limitation. The system treats emotional discharge as inherently corrective, offering little guidance for integration after release. Ritual concludes with catharsis, but the text provides no sustained method for metabolizing the resulting psychological material. The practitioner is expected to return to ordinary life with will strengthened and obstacles diminished, without addressing how repeated ritualization may reshape identity.

This omission has consequences. When ritual becomes the primary means of resolving frustration or asserting control, it risks displacing reflective adaptation. Emotional intensity substitutes for discernment. The practitioner learns to solve problems through escalation rather than recalibration. Over time, the ritual chamber becomes a necessary condition for agency rather than a temporary scaffold.

Sociological analyses of ritualized empowerment systems document a similar pattern. Techniques designed to restore autonomy through symbolic action often produce dependency when they lack mechanisms for post-ritual integration (Dyrendal et al., 2015). The Book of Belial exemplifies this risk. It assumes that will, once strengthened, will naturally self-regulate. The possibility that will may harden into compulsion is not considered.

Laycock observes that Laveyan Satanism consistently equates intensity with authenticity and decisiveness with maturity (Laycock, 2015). In the Book of Belial, this equation becomes operational doctrine. The practitioner is encouraged to act forcefully, decisively, and without ambivalence. Yet ambivalence is not always weakness; it is often a signal of complexity requiring navigation rather than domination.

As with earlier sections, the issue is not efficacy but scope. Greater magic can function as a transitional technology, particularly for individuals emerging from passivity or learned helplessness. It trains focus, legitimizes desire, and counters moral paralysis. The problem arises when ritualized will becomes a permanent orientation. In that case, flexibility diminishes and responsiveness is replaced by repetition.

The Book of Belial offers no criteria for discerning when ritual is no longer adaptive. There is no language for restraint that is not interpreted as retreat, nor for surrender that does not read as defeat. As a result, the practitioner may escalate ritual engagement even as circumstances call for patience, negotiation, or revision of goals.

This pattern deepens the enclosure already present in rupture and lesser magic. Identity becomes organized around forceful intention rather than adaptive intelligence. The practitioner remains powerful but increasingly rigid, capable of decisive action yet less able to respond to nuance or change.

The Book of Belial therefore completes the operational triad of Laveyan Satanism. Rupture breaks inherited authority, lesser magic secures social leverage, and greater magic consolidates will through ritual. Together they produce a self that is autonomous, energized, and defended. What they do not produce is a self capable of modulation once opposition and assertion cease to be necessary.

This chapter does not dismiss ritual or will. It situates them developmentally. Greater magic is effective as scaffolding for agency, not as a permanent mode of engagement with reality. When ritual replaces reflection and intensity substitutes for integration, mastery curdles into compulsion.

Understanding the Book of Belial in these terms clarifies its role within the system. It amplifies power while narrowing range, reinforcing the enclosure that emerges when liberation technologies are mistaken for complete philosophies of life.

Chapter Six

The Book of Leviathan – Ritual as Cathartic Theater and Affective Technology

The *Book of Leviathan* presents the most formally ritualized material in *The Satanic Bible*. It contains Lavey's adaptation of the Enochian keys alongside invocations for lust, compassion, destruction, and a general call. Unlike the *Book of Satan*, which operates through rhetorical rupture, or the *Book of Belial*, which frames ritual as a tool for earthly mastery, the *Book of Leviathan* foregrounds ritual as affective technology: a structured method for inducing, amplifying, and discharging emotion through performance.

Lavey explicitly denies supernatural interpretation of these rituals. The Enochian language is stripped of angelology, cosmology, and theistic metaphysics. Instead, the keys are presented as sonic instruments whose efficacy depends entirely on the emotional authenticity and intensity of the practitioner (Lavey, 1969). Petersen situates this approach within Laveyan Satanism's broader rejection of transcendence, arguing that ritual functions here as psychodrama rather than invocation, with symbolic power directed inward rather than outward (Petersen, 2008).

From a performance-theory perspective, the *Book of Leviathan* is the clearest expression of Lavey's background in theatrical staging and affect manipulation. The ritual chamber, lighting, vocal cadence, and timing are all designed to bypass discursive cognition and activate limbic response. Dyrendal, Lewis, and Petersen describe these rituals as "cathartic theater," emphasizing that their primary function is emotional discharge and identity reinforcement rather than metaphysical efficacy (Dyrendal et al., 2015).

The Enochian keys play a central role in this theater. Their archaic diction and infernal imagery operate as mnemonic triggers that heighten arousal and concentrate attention. Linguistically opaque and rhythmically forceful, the keys bypass semantic processing and act directly on affective circuits. Research on ritualized language across traditions supports this interpretation, showing that non-semantic or partially opaque language can intensify emotional response by disengaging critical evaluation (Farias & Wikholm, 2015).

Practitioners frequently report powerful subjective effects following invocation: clarity, reduced muscular tension, emotional relief, and renewed agency. These outcomes align with broader findings in trauma and affect regulation research, where controlled catharsis can temporarily reduce anxiety and restore a sense of control when emotion has been chronically suppressed (Farias & Wikholm, 2015). Lavey's rituals provide a container for such release, allowing rage, lust, or compassion to be expressed without immediate social consequence.

The structure of the *Book of Leviathan* reinforces this containment. Each ritual follows a similar arc: preparation, invocation, emotional escalation, discharge, and closure. This arc mirrors classical models of ritual efficacy in which boundaries prevent affective overflow and preserve ego coherence. When practiced episodically, such containment can be stabilizing.

However, the *Book of Leviathan* offers no explicit instruction for integration after discharge. Emotional release is treated as sufficient in itself. The text assumes that catharsis restores balance and that the practitioner will naturally recalibrate. Empirical research suggests otherwise. Farias and Wikholm document that repeated induction of altered or peak states without reflective processing can lead to emotional dependency, dysregulation, and avoidance of deeper psychological work (Farias & Wikholm, 2015).

This risk is especially pronounced given the solitary nature of Laveyan ritual practice. Group ritual is deemphasized; invocation is typically conducted alone. While this preserves autonomy, it also limits feedback. Without interpersonal correction, practitioners may misattribute relief to ritual performance rather than to transient physiological effects or behavioral change. Hassan's work on high-control systems highlights how internal architectures built from system categories can be experienced as personal strength even as they narrow perception and choice (Hassan, 1990).

The three primary ritual types—lust, compassion, and destruction—each activate distinct affective configurations. Lust rituals mobilize sexual arousal; compassion rituals amplify empathic affect; destruction rituals channel rage. Jungian shadow theory provides a useful analytic lens here. Each ritual calls forth material that is often repressed or moralized in mainstream culture. The ritual container allows temporary access without overt identification.

Problems arise when access becomes identification. Shadow inflation occurs when the practitioner begins to define identity through the activated state rather than integrating it into a broader self-structure. In the context of the *Book of Leviathan*, this manifests as compulsive repetition. Practitioners chase the emotional peak rather than cultivating stability. Catharsis becomes maintenance.

31

Vedantic guna theory clarifies this dynamic at an energetic level. The rituals of the *Book of Leviathan* are heavily rajasic in their arousal and activation, with tamasic elements introduced through repetition, fixation, and symbolic density. Sattvic qualities—clarity, rest, and integration—are briefly accessed during post-ritual calm but are not systematically cultivated (Puligandla, 1975).

Psychometric research on guna profiles supports the predictive value of this model. Rajasic and tamasic dominance correlates with elevated stress and reduced well-being, while sustained sattvic balance correlates with psychological resilience (Wolf, 1999; Krishnan, 2022). Repeated cathartic discharge without integration amplifies rajas and tamas while eroding sattva. The practitioner feels powerful yet increasingly brittle.

The atheistic framing of Laveyan Satanism intensifies this risk. By rejecting supernatural narratives, the system removes external interpretive buffers. There is no cosmology to contextualize failure or excess. When relief fades, the practitioner is encouraged—implicitly if not explicitly—to increase intensity rather than to pause. Emotional authenticity becomes the sole criterion of efficacy.

From a chaos magick perspective—again used here as an analytic lens rather than an influence claim—the Enochian keys function as temporary paradigm tools. The practitioner installs belief long enough for affect and behavior to shift, ideally releasing it afterward. The *Book of Leviathan* provides installation but not release. Without metacognitive awareness, belief hardens into compulsion.

Socially, the effects are isolating. Ritual practice becomes a private source of meaning and regulation, reducing reliance on relational engagement. Emotional discharge occurs in a vacuum rather than through dialogue, repair, or shared vulnerability. Relationships may atrophy as ritual substitutes for connection. Empirical studies of Satanist identity note similar tensions between autonomy and belonging, with solitary practice amplifying both independence and alienation (Sprankle et al., 2019).

The *Book of Leviathan* thus occupies a critical position in Lavey's system. It delivers the most intense affective payoff while also introducing the highest risk of dependency. Catharsis feels transformative and invites repetition. Without integration, the theater begins to own the actor. Invocations that once liberated emotion begin to dictate behavior.

This chapter does not deny the genuine benefits of ritual catharsis. For individuals with repressed emotion or unresolved anger, the *Book of Leviathan* can provide relief that feels life-saving. The problem is not that the rituals work. The problem is that the system offers no criteria for sufficiency, no guidance for stopping, and no pathway beyond discharge.

Understanding the *Book of Leviathan* as affective technology rather than as mystical practice clarifies both its power and its limits. Ritual stabilizes the psyche long enough for intent to form, but stabilization without integration produces dependency. The next chapter examines how Lavey's system structurally frames integration itself as weakness, completing the arc from liberation to enclosure.

Chapter Seven

Integration Framed as Weakness – The Enclosure Completed

This chapter argues that Lavey's system structurally frames integration—understood here as permeability, receptivity, and the capacity to be altered by experience without loss of agency—as weakness. This framing is not an oversight or rhetorical excess. It is a functional necessity for a philosophy organized around permanent opposition. A system that derives coherence from rupture must define anything that threatens rupture as hostile, and integration presents the most direct threat of all.

Integration allows previously rejected material to re-enter awareness without surrendering authorship or agency. That possibility destabilizes the binary logic on which Laveyan Satanism depends. The system therefore cannot acknowledge integration as a legitimate developmental capacity without undermining its own foundation. As a result, integration is preemptively coded as capitulation rather than maturity.

Across *The Satanic Bible*, strength is consistently defined in terms of resistance, refusal, and self-containment. Softness, receptivity, and emotional permeability are framed as vulnerabilities that invite domination. This evaluative pattern operates less at the level of explicit doctrine than at the level of somatic conditioning. Long before integration is considered as an idea, the practitioner is trained to experience openness as danger. The body learns to flinch.

Scholars of Laveyan Satanism have noted this asymmetry repeatedly. Dyrendal, Lewis, and Petersen describe the system as privileging antagonism and self-assertion while offering little language for reconciliation or synthesis (Dyrendal et al., 2015). Laycock similarly observes that Satanic identity is stabilized through oppositional narrative rather than through shared belief or relational depth (Laycock, 2015). Opposition provides cohesion; permeability threatens it.

This structural bias has predictable developmental consequences. Erikson's theory of identity formation provides a useful baseline. Erikson distinguishes between necessary periods of rupture and experimentation—what he terms "moratorium"—and foreclosure, the premature fixation of identity that resists revision (Erikson, 1968). Rupture is developmentally intelligible; foreclosure is limiting. Lavey's system facilitates rupture but provides no pathway beyond it. What begins as moratorium hardens into foreclosure.

Research on world-rejecting movements supports this trajectory. Black's qualitative study of former members demonstrates that systems organized around sharp rupture often function as temporary solutions to crises of autonomy and belonging, with later exit driven by the need to integrate independence with relational connection (Black, 2011). Where integration is framed as betrayal, practitioners face a binary choice: double down on defense or abandon the system entirely.

Laveyan Satanism does not explicitly forbid exit, but it renders integration unintelligible. Adjustment is interpreted as weakness;

listening is framed as vulnerability rather than perception; yielding is equated with defeat. Agency becomes synonymous with imposition rather than navigation. In this frame, intelligence is measured by refusal, not by responsiveness.

The social effects follow immediately. Because integration is coded as weakness, any attempt to revise posture in response to experience risks social demotion within the system's implicit hierarchy. Hardness is rewarded with recognition; openness invites suspicion. This produces a feedback loop in which rigidity is reinforced both personally and socially. Identity stabilizes around what cannot change rather than around what can adapt.

Critical social theory offers language for this dynamic. Horkheimer and Adorno argue that projects of emancipation aimed at rational self-mastery can solidify into new forms of domination when controlling logics are internalized and experienced as freedom (Horkheimer & Adorno, 2002). The subject believes himself liberated precisely because control has moved inside. Ritzer's reformulation of Weber's "iron cage" similarly shows how rationalized systems promise efficiency and mastery while producing environments of constraint that practitioners both rely on and feel trapped within (Ritzer, 1993).

In Lavey's system, the iron cage is not imposed by bureaucracy or doctrine but by identity. The practitioner internalizes a posture of perpetual defense. Strength is measured by impermeability. Over time, this posture becomes exhausting. Early gains in autonomy and clarity give way to repetition. The system offers no new direction beyond the refinement of defense. Refinement replaces development.

This exhaustion is not immediately recognized as pathology. It is reframed as realism. Absence of wonder, surprise, or deep satisfaction becomes normalized as maturity. Longing is treated as nostalgia for outgrown illusions. Vitality is quietly redefined downward. Bauman's analysis of liquid modernity clarifies why this redefinition can feel necessary. In unstable social conditions, solidity—even brittle solidity—can feel safer than openness (Bauman, 2000).

Yet vitality is not a luxury. Psychological research consistently shows that well-being depends on both agency and receptivity. Without the capacity to be affected, the subject cannot be nourished by experience. Desire, creativity, and time itself begin to narrow. Desire becomes repetitive rather than exploratory; creativity shifts from exploration to execution; time becomes linear and accumulative rather than rhythmic.

Vedantic guna theory provides a diagnostic lens for this narrowing. Lavey's system is heavily rajasic and tamasic: driven, oppositional, and resistant. Sattva—clarity without reactivity, rest without collapse, integration without surrender—is conspicuously absent as a cultivated capacity. Contemporary psychometric research supports the predictive value of this model. Rajasic and tamasic dominance correlates with elevated stress and reduced life satisfaction, while sattvic balance correlates with resilience and well-being (Wolf, 1999; Krishnan, 2022).

The absence of sattva explains why the system delivers explosive liberation followed by chronic arousal. Rajas breaks chains; tamas anchors identity; without sattva, there is no return to equilibrium. The subject remains upright but undernourished—powerful yet brittle.

Clinical and phenomenological observation reinforces this account. Practitioners often report that Laveyan techniques saved them from pathological guilt, coercive religiosity, or learned helplessness. The rupture phase is experienced as life-giving. Years later, the same practitioners describe living inside a fortress of their own construction. The structure keeps threats out but also keeps possibility from entering. What once functioned as liberation becomes enclosure.

This enclosure reshapes desire at its root. Desire, initially sharpened by the dissolution of guilt, becomes something to be managed rather than followed. The subject delays desire, brackets it, and deploys it strategically. Experiences that cannot be defended or justified within the system's logic are excluded from consideration. Over time, fluency in wanting anything that requires exposure or reorientation is lost.

Creativity deteriorates through the same mechanism. Creative work requires willingness to be altered by material, process, failure, and the unknown. A system that prizes certainty and control treats these conditions as threats. Competence remains; renewal does not. The subject produces without being fed by production.

Relationally, integration framed as weakness limits the degree to which others are allowed to matter. Even valued relationships are kept within boundaries that prevent mutual transformation. Interaction becomes management. Shared vulnerability is avoided. Many forms of meaning that arise only through co-creation and responsiveness never emerge.

Importantly, none of this requires malevolence or manipulation. The enclosure is structural. A philosophy built on permanent opposition cannot accommodate permeability without dissolving itself. The system solved the problem it was designed to solve—liberation from imposed authority—and then insisted no further problems existed.

Integration threatens this insistence. Integration would reveal rupture as phase rather than destination. It would show that autonomy can coexist with receptivity and that strength need not require impermeability. For this reason, integration is rendered embarrassing rather than debated. Embarrassment bypasses rational evaluation and appeals directly to identity maintenance.

This chapter does not argue for reconciliation with rejected authority, nor for a return to what was escaped. Integration is not surrender. It is structural maturity: the capacity to remain intact while being altered by experience. It preserves authorship while expanding responsiveness.

A mature self can deploy refusal without requiring it as identity. Opposition loses centrality. Energy is freed for creation, navigation, and renewal. The self is no longer sustained by what it resists but by what sustains it.

This distinction is absent from Lavey's rhetoric but unavoidable in lived reality. Freedom, understood developmentally, is not a static condition but a practice. It must adapt as circumstances change. A self that cannot revise its own structures becomes captive to them regardless of how those structures were formed.

Chapter Seven completes the diagnostic arc of Book One. The system's brilliance lies in its capacity to rupture. Its failure lies in its refusal of integration. What remains is not condemnation but clarity: recognition of where the tool ends and the cage begins.

The next movement concerns orientation rather than critique—how a self forged through rupture can live without reproducing captivity in elegant form.

CONCLUSION

Bridge: From Rupture to Integration

Book One completes the forensic interview by following Lavey's system from its origins through its core operations and into the point where liberation begins to harden into enclosure. The analysis traces how rupture functions effectively during specific phases of development and how those same mechanisms begin to fail when treated as permanent identity.

What Lavey never named, and what systems like his structurally cannot name without undoing themselves, is the observer beneath the posture. His text teaches identification with the adversarial stance but provides no mechanism for stepping out of that identification once rupture succeeds. Without that capacity, the practitioner mistakes the stance for awakening and the armor for strength.

This omission is not unique to Laveyan Satanism. It appears wherever rupture is treated as destination rather than phase. The pattern recurs: a system delivers real liberation from one enclosure, then quietly installs another through the same mechanisms that produced freedom. Integration is framed as weakness. Permeability is coded as surrender.

The result is practitioners who are potent but undernourished, autonomous but isolated.

Book Two does not offer a replacement system. It provides diagnostic frameworks that make the enclosure visible and tools for recognizing where identification is operating. These frameworks, drawn from Solomonic containment architecture, Vedantic witness practice, phenomenological cartography, and philosophical accounts of responsibility, are not doctrines to adopt. They are lenses that reveal what happens when symbolic power reorganizes identity without teaching observers how to step back from what they have become.

The work ahead is not to repudiate rupture or return to what was escaped. The work is to complete what rupture could not: the recognition that even the stance of liberation is still a stance, and something must remain distinct enough to see it.

Beyond the Break: Criteria for Continuation

The interrogation of Anton Lavey's *The Satanic Bible* has reached the limits of what critique alone can accomplish. Seven chapters have traced the system's architecture from biographical origins through the Nine Statements, across the four Books, and into the final enclosure where liberation hardens into elegant captivity. The pattern that emerges is consistent and repeatable. A technology designed for rupture succeeds brilliantly at its assigned task while systematically refusing to acknowledge that the task is phase-limited rather than terminal.

What remains is not synthesis. The book has argued throughout that synthesis would repeat Lavey's error of claiming finality. What remains instead is orientation. For readers who recognize themselves in these pages, who have lived the arc from empowerment to constraint, the question necessarily shifts from analysis to application.

The system's core limitation is structural rather than accidental. A philosophy organized entirely around opposition to external authority cannot develop language for maturity beyond defense without undermining its own coherence. Capacities essential for sustained life, including integration, permeability, and responsiveness, are therefore coded as weakness. Acknowledging these capacities as strengths would reveal rupture as incomplete rather than terminal.

Lavey built a manual for breaking chains rather than a map for learning to walk unchained. This distinction does not indicate failure. It indicates scope. Failure occurs only when practitioners mistake the manual for a comprehensive philosophy of life.

That mistake emerges when defense against coercion is confused with a blueprint for living. The rage that shattered inherited guilt is preserved decades after the original threat has passed. At that point, the system stops serving and begins owning. The practitioner becomes maintenance staff for machinery installed during crisis.

Recognition of this dynamic does not require abandoning what the system provided. The permissions articulated in the Nine Statements remain valid. Indulgence counters pathological denial, vital existence counters spiritual escapism, and undefiled wisdom counters self-deception. These gains do not disappear when the system's limits are acknowledged.

The rupture enacted by the Book of Satan remains necessary for many practitioners trapped in coercive morality. Lesser magic's tactical intelligence and greater magic's ritual technology continue to function as designed. What must be relinquished is the claim that these tools constitute a complete philosophy. Rupture must be understood as intervention rather than destination.

This shift is one of contextualization rather than reversal. It involves understanding the system as a powerful, phase-specific technology rather than terminal truth. The shift feels dangerous because it threatens identity stability built through years of boundary enforcement. Refusing the shift, however, produces costs that accumulate silently.

These costs include erosion of vitality, creative stagnation, relational thinning, and temporal flattening. The self remains defended but increasingly isolated from sources of renewal and meaning. Strength persists, but nourishment does not. The enclosure becomes elegant precisely because it feels earned.

Three criteria reliably indicate readiness for movement beyond the system's limits. The first criterion appears when techniques that once produced clarity and power begin yielding diminishing returns. Boundary enforcement that secured autonomy begins generating isolation rather than freedom. Practices that once felt liberating now feel obligatory.

Selectivity that once conserved energy produces scarcity of connection. Refusal that once established sovereignty begins to feel reflexive rather than chosen. When practices originally deployed to escape captivity begin reproducing similar constraint, the system has completed its useful phase. Continuation becomes maintenance.

The second criterion appears when desire flattens despite maintained intensity. Goals pursued with fierce commitment no longer resonate upon achievement. Victories accumulate without altering the internal landscape. Stimulation escalates while satisfaction remains elusive.

This pattern signals that will remains functional but has lost permeability. The self can still impose direction but can no longer be

43

nourished by what it encounters. Intensity replaces responsiveness. Desire circulates without renewal.

The third criterion appears in relational patterns. Relationships stabilize around transaction, performance, or controlled distance rather than mutual transformation. Others are engaged tactically or kept at arm's length. Even valued connections operate within boundaries that prevent genuine risk.

Loneliness persists despite social activity. The isolation does not arise from lack of contact but from absence of permeability. Interaction occurs without being affected. Connection is managed rather than inhabited.

These criteria do not suggest regression to pre-rupture states. A practitioner who has genuinely integrated the system's permissions cannot return to naive submission or uncritical acceptance of authority. The dismantling of guilt, reclamation of agency, and establishment of boundaries remain valid achievements. What must develop is capacity rather than reversal.

What must develop is a capacity for discrimination the system never cultivated. The practitioner must learn when to enforce boundaries and when to allow permeability. The practitioner must learn when to impose will and when to navigate through responsiveness. These discriminations were structurally excluded by the system.

These discriminations require tolerance for states the system trained the practitioner to avoid. Such states include uncertainty without immediate resolution, ambiguity without forced clarity, and receptivity without collapse into weakness. Tolerance for these states does not indicate softness. It indicates expanded range.

Strength that includes only hardness is brittle. Strength that can modulate between resistance and responsiveness is durable. Durability, not dominance, determines longevity.

Movement beyond rupture does not follow a prescribed path. Prescribed paths reproduce the problem they claim to solve. What can be offered instead are structural capacities that allow life to remain coherent while permitting evolution. These capacities do not dictate outcomes.

Permeability without surrender refers to the capacity to be affected by experience, relationship, failure, and beauty without losing authorship. This capacity depends on internal differentiation rather than external defense. The self must be able to take in information, evaluate it against values and purpose, integrate what serves, and release what does not.

Will understood as navigation rather than imposition refers to the capacity to adjust direction based on encountered conditions while maintaining orientation. This form of will allows learning from resistance rather than only overcoming it. Yielding in this context does not signify defeat. Yielding signifies intelligent responsiveness.

Integration understood as structural maturity refers to the capacity to hold contradictory impulses, unresolved affects, and ambiguous meanings without forcing immediate resolution through dominance or dismissal. This tolerance allows the self to be informed by its own complexity rather than continually editing experience to fit a single posture. Integration stabilizes authorship rather than dissolving it.

These capacities do not arise from techniques in the sense Lavey's system provides. They develop through sustained engagement with situations that demand them. Such situations include relationships requiring vulnerability without guarantees, creative work that resists control, encounters with beauty or suffering that refuse reduction, and failures that cannot be dismissed.

The practitioner forged in rupture often avoids precisely these situations because they threaten identity stabilized around defense. Avoidance ensures stagnation. Growth occurs at the edges of competence rather than at the center of mastery. Remaining at the center produces refinement without renewal.

For practitioners still living inside the system, several recognitions may prove useful. The first recognition involves acknowledging without guilt that what once saved you may now constrain you. Systems are phase-specific, and outgrowing one is maturation rather than betrayal. No loyalty is owed to a tool beyond its usefulness.

The second recognition involves distinguishing between boundaries that serve life and boundaries that define identity. Boundaries are tools rather than essence. When preservation of posture becomes more important than quality of life, the boundary has become a cage. The distinction becomes visible only when costs accumulate.

The third recognition involves experimenting with selective permeability in low-risk contexts. Allow another perspective to register as information rather than threat. Permit uncertainty to exist without forcing immediate action. Observe whether agency collapses or expands.

Most practitioners discover that selective openness expands agency rather than diminishing it. Sovereignty becomes interactive rather than defensive. Strength becomes contextual rather than rigid. Control loosens without disappearing.

For scholars examining systems like Lavey's, the pattern identified here applies broadly. Any philosophy organized around liberation from coercion faces the same risk. Rupture mechanisms that free can become identity structures that constrain. The more effective the rupture, the more seductive the enclosure.

Relief is attributed to the system's totality rather than to its specific rupture function. Identity stabilizes around defense, and revision becomes threatening. Recognizing this pattern requires distinguishing tool efficacy from philosophical completeness. A system can function brilliantly for its designed purpose while remaining insufficient as a comprehensive life model.

What lies beyond rupture remains open. This book has argued that Lavey's system cannot answer that question without undermining itself. Integration is structurally foreclosed by the logic of permanent opposition. What follows rupture is therefore not Lavey's domain.

What follows rupture is the practitioner's work. That work cannot be prescribed because prescriptions would install new enclosures. What can be stated is that maturity beyond defense requires capacities the system does not cultivate. These capacities include permeability without collapse, navigation without loss of direction, integration without fragmentation, and responsiveness without submission.

These capacities emerge through engagement with complexity rather than through technique. The practitioner must risk being changed. Without that risk, the practitioner remains frozen at the moment of rupture regardless of skill. Stasis disguises itself as mastery.

The "prison interview" metaphor captures a specific recognition. The practitioner inside the system cannot see the walls because the walls are built from the inside and labeled as strength. Maintenance feels like liberation, narrowing feels like refinement, and isolation feels like sovereignty. The enclosure becomes invisible because it is self-authored.

External critique is dismissed as weakness. Yet signals accumulate beneath maintained intensity. Diminishing returns, flattened desire, relational thinning, and exhaustion begin to register. These signals are not moral failures but structural indicators.

The interview does not provide escape. It provides recognition. Recognition establishes that the cage exists even when invisible. That recognition is the precondition for choice.

Without recognition, the practitioner continues maintaining machinery installed during crisis. Competence at defense is mistaken for mastery of life. The system continues to function exactly as designed. The cost continues to accrue.

For those who have lived the pattern, this book offers neither redemption nor a new system. It offers language for what is already known. It offers criteria for recognizing when transition becomes necessary. It offers permission to acknowledge that outgrowing a system that once saved you is a developmental necessity.

The work ahead is yours. The system taught defense brilliantly. Learning to live beyond defense requires different teachers. Experience, relationships that resist technique, failures that cannot be dismissed, and encounters with complexity provide those lessons.

Anton Lavey built a manual for breaking chains. That achievement remains legitimate. For those still bound by guilt or imposed morality, the manual retains full power. Its usefulness does not vanish because its limits are acknowledged.

Chains, however, break quickly. Life continues for decades. Mistaking the manual for the entirety of freedom is the final trap. This trap is more elegant than what was escaped because it is chosen.

This book has attempted to map that trap with precision. The exit is not a prescribed path. The exit is structural capacity. Whether to develop that capacity, when to begin, and how to proceed remain your questions. The observer was never at stake. What you do, now that you see, is. Book Two examines the architectural safeguards that older traditions provided and modern rupture grimoires omit: the tools that allow symbolic contact without possession, observation without identification, and power without capture. The prison interview is complete. What follows is your responsibility.

BOOK TWO

Chapter One

Symbolic Power and the Unscaffolded Grimoire

Lavey's system demonstrated with unusual clarity what happens when symbolic power is granted without scaffolding. Book One traced that mechanism through his text. What follows is an examination of the tools he never provided, not to replace his system, but to reveal the architecture that older traditions understood and modern rupture grimoires omit.

One caveat has emerged repeatedly in my research and long-form investigation of initiatory systems, and it is something novices cannot yet see. The left-hand path is not inherently dangerous in a moral sense. The danger lies in what is not taught alongside its tools, particularly in modern Satanic texts that function less as theology than as applied psychological magick. The Satanic Bible, as written by Anton Lavey, is effective precisely because it bypasses belief and works directly on conditioning, affect, and will. It alters posture toward guilt, authority, and agency without requiring metaphysical assent. That is its strength.

The recurring problem across Satanic grimoires of genuine value is not incompetence but incompleteness. These texts hand the reader a loaded weapon and indicate where to pull, without providing groundwork, containment, developmental sequencing, or post-activation integration. There is no instruction on how to hold the tool safely, no pacing for when symbolic force begins to respond, and no guidance for what follows once rupture succeeds. Power is granted without calibration. Agency is unlocked without context.

Whether this omission is accidental or deliberate is ultimately irrelevant. What matters operationally is the outcome. These texts reliably produce rupture, often quickly and decisively. They break guilt, dissolve external authority, and restore a sense of force to individuals who have been disempowered, constrained, or chronically self-doubting. The practitioner feels clearer, sharper, more honest, and less willing to tolerate internal contradiction. What is rarely addressed is what comes next.

Rupture does not arrive as chaos. It arrives as relief.

For many practitioners, the initial phase is characterized by an unmistakable sense of correctness. Long-standing internal friction falls away. Decisions feel easier. Moral ambiguity collapses into certainty. Authority structures, religious, familial, and cultural, lose their grip almost overnight. This is experienced not as rebellion but as realism. The world appears less sentimental and more legible. People who resist this shift appear weak, dishonest, or asleep.

This is the point at which many mistake rupture for integration.

Social consequences follow quickly. Relationships reorganize around new boundaries. Some fall away. Others harden into adversarial patterns. The practitioner may find themselves increasingly isolated, not because they seek isolation, but because their interpretive frame has narrowed. Disagreement no longer feels neutral. It feels diagnostic.

Opposition becomes confirmation. The practitioner begins to identify not only with a new value set but with the posture of opposition itself.

Internally, the aftertaste of rupture is rarely peace. It is alertness, a low-grade readiness, a sense that clarity must be maintained through tension. Stillness begins to feel suspect, even threatening. The practitioner does not feel possessed. They feel awake. And because the change feels real, because it is real in its effects, it becomes difficult to question.

The critique taken here is therefore not that the weapon exists, nor that it fires, nor that rupture is illegitimate. The critique is instructional. No one explains recoil. No one explains aim. No one explains what happens when there is no longer a target. The reader is taught how to pull the trigger but not how to live afterward, especially once the world begins to respond.

To understand why this matters, one principle must be stated plainly. The power of symbol in magical systems is not incidental. It is foundational. Symbols are not representations of magick in the way diagrams represent machines. In practice, they are the machine. They act where conscious skepticism has the least leverage and where identity is formed most efficiently. They act in the mind, and more specifically in the layers of mind that do not speak in linear language.

From a psychological perspective, the subconscious is not a poetic abstraction. It is the accumulated structure of impressions the nervous system has registered over a lifetime: affective tone, threat calibration, reward expectancy, bodily posture, and associative memory. Long before deliberate choice appears, this substrate is already biasing perception and steering behavior. Volition does not arise in a vacuum. It emerges downstream from conditioning, pattern recognition, and affective momentum that operate largely outside awareness. In that sense, the subconscious does not merely support identity. It precedes it.

Despite its complexity, the subconscious operates with remarkable economy. Across depth psychology and early cognitive theory, one working hypothesis recurs with enough consistency to be operationally useful: the subconscious communicates primarily through image rather than through linear language. Images compress information. A single symbolic image can carry emotional tone, memory, bodily sensation, narrative implication, and motivational force simultaneously. Words unfold sequentially. Images transmit all at once.

The conscious mind speaks in sentences. The subconscious answers in pictures, sensations, and symbolic associations. Most people never learn to bridge that gap deliberately.

This is precisely where magical systems intervene.

What the magician is learning beneath ritual language and dramatic framing is a symbolic vocabulary the subconscious already understands. Elements, archetypes, sigils, gestures, colors, and names function as a structured language that bypasses rational dispute and speaks directly to associative depth. Patterns accumulate. Affect binds to form. The practitioner feeds the psyche material in a format it recognizes. The result is not supernatural causation as a violation of physics. It is communication with the parts of mind that govern attention, motivation, and meaning before conscious narration begins.

Stripped of fantasy and theatrics, the most defensible operational definition of magick is not metaphysical power but engineered synchronicity. It is intervention at the junction where meaning, perception, probability, and action converge. Anything less collapses into optimism or self-help by another name. Anything more implies a causal claim about physical law. Synchronicity occupies the narrow and unsettling middle ground, where shifts in attention, interpretation, risk tolerance, and behavior can produce real increases in meaningful coincidence without invoking supernatural mechanics.

This definition matters because it returns directly to the danger embedded in certain Satanic and left-hand path grimoires. These texts do not promise vague spiritual growth. They promise leverage. They assert, implicitly or explicitly, that by manipulating symbol, affect, and will, the practitioner can bend outcomes by influencing the web of perception and response in which events unfold.

When that works, even partially, it is intoxicating.

Coincidence tightens into narrative. Attention sharpens around confirming details. The practitioner notices patterns they would previously have ignored. Behavior subtly shifts to meet opportunity. Risk tolerance increases. Agency feels restored. None of this requires delusion. It requires only reinforcement. The world begins to appear responsive not because it has changed metaphysically but because perception has been reweighted.

Without containment, this acceleration becomes indistinguishable from revelation.

From a depth-psychological perspective, this is where trouble becomes predictable. Symbol does not merely represent ideas; it mobilizes. Once activated, symbolic material carries emotional charge, bodily response, and behavioral momentum. These forces do not politely retreat when the ritual ends. They reorganize perception and action downstream. If coincidences cluster, whether through sharpened attention, altered behavior, or genuine chance, the practitioner experiences confirmation. The narrative tightens. Meaning accelerates.

At that point, fantasy is no longer the issue. The issue is premature causality attribution.

The practitioner is taught how to load the weapon and fire it, but not how to recognize recoil, misfire, or collateral damage. There is no instruction for what happens when the symbolic system begins to feed back on itself, when coincidence reinforces belief, and belief sharpens perception until the world appears responsive and oppositional. The practitioner has learned to speak to the subconscious fluently but has not learned how to listen, regulate, or stop.

This is why grounding in physiology matters, not to reduce the phenomenon to biology but to explain why it persists. The nervous system does not distinguish cleanly between imagined threat, symbolic meaning, and immediate physical danger. Once a pattern is registered as salient, the body responds as if it were real. Repeated activation recruits threat and reward circuits simultaneously. What appears to work is reinforced. Attention sharpens. Pattern recognition accelerates.

Over time, this conditioning becomes embodied. Stress hormones mobilize action. Reinforcement binds efficacy to symbolic posture. Defensive readiness becomes habit. Calm begins to feel wrong. Stillness reads as danger. This is not belief. It is training. The body learns the stance the symbol demands.

Seen this way, the danger of the Satanic grimoire is no longer moral or theological. It is instructional. Power is activated without education. Symbol is mobilized without grammar. Synchronicity is engineered without discernment. The gun fires, recoil and all, and the practitioner is left to learn after the fact what has already been set in motion.

That is the threshold this book addresses.

What follows is not a condemnation of rupture, nor a retreat into moral restraint. It is an examination of what earlier systems quietly understood and modern ones omit: if symbolic power is real in its effects, then something must exist that can encounter it without being consumed by it.

The next chapter turns to the first architecture built to solve that problem.

Chapter Two

The Mirror and the Demon: Containment, Contact, and the Refusal of Possession

Before turning toward integration, it is necessary to linger with a Western tradition that already understood, long before psychology supplied terminology, that symbolic power is not merely persuasive but destabilizing. Solomonic magic matters here not because Solomon is a reliable historical author, nor because the grimoires deserve reverence, but because the tradition repeatedly encodes one operational safeguard: contact is permissible; identification is not. In Solomonic method, the magician is not invited to become a vessel, an oracle, or a mouthpiece for the forces he stirs, but is required to remain an operator, which in practical terms means remaining an observer with boundaries intact. That insistence is not aesthetic. It is diagnostic. Symbolic encounter can reorganize the psyche faster than conscious intention can stabilize it, and without enforced differentiation, contact collapses into fusion.

The circle, the triangle, and the mirror are therefore not stage props but instruments for preserving differentiation. The circle defines the position of the operator and declares that this position is not negotiable once the work begins, while the triangle defines the position of the force as something constrained, questioned, and released on terms that protect the whole system. The mirror, when it appears, performs a subtler function by making the force visible without allowing fusion and forcing the magician to relate to what appears rather than collapse into it. Modern readers often dismiss this architecture as medieval superstition, but it is more accurately read as crude and effective metacognitive hygiene. The structure holds the symbolic encounter at a distance where choice remains possible.

The Goetic spirits sharpen this insight because they are not treated as gods or teachers but as narrow competencies described in personal terms. Their defining feature is functional intensity rather than wholeness, with one governing deception, another persuasion, another lust, another destruction, and another secrecy. None are praised for wisdom, patience, or restraint, because the tradition does not pretend they possess these qualities. Their utility lies precisely in their specialization, and their danger lies there as well. A single-function intelligence, once allowed to dominate, cannot preserve the larger ecology of the self, because it will do its job efficiently while narrowing the system that hosts it.

This is why Solomonic texts place such weight on beginning and ending, on purifications, constraints, conjurations, and licenses to depart. These formalities are not moral posturing but containment technology designed to prevent drift. The magician is not taught to bask in the presence of the force or to treat the encounter as proof of personal destiny, but to begin deliberately, keep the force located, and end cleanly. Even in the most theatrical versions of the tradition, the operative message remains consistent: do not let the thing you called become the thing you are.

When psychology later developed language for the unconscious, it described a parallel structure using different terms. In Jungian psychology, the shadow is not a single dark impulse but a constellation of disowned capacities split off because they conflicted with the conscious identity. These fragments do not disappear, and when activated they behave like internal agents with their own affective charge and momentum. If ignored, they intrude; if projected, they appear as enemies outside; and if embraced without containment, they inflate the ego. The core danger is not that the shadow exists, but that the ego mistakes contact for mastery and confuses intensity with integration.

Where modern grimoires often go wrong is not that they touch these forces, but that they remove the very architecture designed to prevent possession. Rupture-oriented systems, particularly modern left-hand path texts, frequently encourage the practitioner to internalize the adversarial posture as identity. The demon is no longer a force in the triangle and the shadow is no longer mirrored, because it is enthroned. In the early phase this feels like liberation, because it restores access to capacities that were previously suppressed and grants the practitioner a coherent narrative of strength. A coherent narrative, however, is not the same thing as a coherent psyche, and the initial gains become a trap precisely because they are real.

This is the point at which Jung's private work becomes conceptually relevant, not as doctrine or occult endorsement, but as a modern demonstration of the same structural risk. In *Liber Novus*, Jung describes being compelled by a deeper current of psyche that did not obey his intellectual preferences and did not ask permission from his professional identity, and he distinguishes the "spirit of the time" from the "spirit of the depths" as incompatible demands placed on the self

(Jung, 2009). That distinction is not philosophical ornament but structural description. The conscious mind wants control and justification. The deeper symbolic strata push material forward with their own authority. Jung's confrontation did not feel like enlightenment, and he framed it as dangerous because the material threatened orientation and tempted identification. What prevented collapse was not belief or repression but method: recording, dialoguing, containing, and returning without obedience.

The parallel becomes sharper when we name what both Solomonic magic and Jungian psychology guard against: the collapse of differentiation. When differentiation collapses, a single psychic mode becomes the whole person, rage becomes clarity, contempt becomes discernment, opposition becomes truth, and coincidence becomes destiny. The practitioner no longer has a relationship to the force because the force becomes the interpretive lens itself. This is the psychological anatomy of possession even if no spirits exist outside the mind. It is also the anatomy of inflation, in which the ego fuses with archetypal material and experiences that fusion as exaltation rather than narrowing. Containment is therefore not an antiquated term but the difference between using a tool and being used by it.

Modern readers often underestimate this danger because they assume meaning is reversible. They imagine that perception can be altered temporarily and then returned to baseline without residue, but the psyche does not operate like a screen that can be cleared at will. Altered states reorganize salience, memory, and interpretation in ways that can persist, whether induced by ritual, imagination, trauma, or pharmacology. This is why initiation systems historically insisted on pacing, framing, and return, because the operator must be able to exit the state cleanly if ordinary life is to remain intact. Where that structure is absent, the nervous system stabilizes by narrowing, filling the gap with certainty and identity rather than choice.

60

Alchemy belongs in this chapter for the same reason, because it treated symbolic work as transformation rather than belief. Classical alchemical language describes death, dissolution, putrefaction, separation, and recombination not as moral metaphors but as the shape of destabilization and reconstitution in lived perception. What is dissolved is not only substance but a way of seeing, and what is recombined is not only matter but meaning. The obsession with vessels, seals, timings, and stages is not mystical ornamentation but containment technology, defining where transformation may occur and where it must not. From this angle, modern rupture grimoires do not look daring. They look impatient.

Papus makes this principle explicit by treating symbolic systems as keys to how consciousness organizes itself rather than as objects of faith. In his framing, symbols act simultaneously on intellectual, emotional, imaginal, and somatic levels. Producing coordinated reorientation rather than mere ideas, and he treats the tarot as operative grammar rather than parlor toy (papus, 1892/2009). This aligns with the structural danger already traced, because symbols that reorganize perception cannot be handled casually. Alchemy refuses immediacy for this reason, treating sudden transformation as catastrophic rather than enlightened, because too much intensity collapses differentiation and produces ash rather than integration.

It is therefore necessary to address the final objection often raised by skeptics, namely that symbols are merely cultural overlays imposed on an otherwise neutral brain. Contemporary cognitive neuroscience does not support this view. Human reversible symbol use recruits a widespread fronto-parietal-temporal network that overlaps higher cognition and language systems, while symbolic meaning engages circuits involved in social cognition and self-representation (Dehaene et al., 2024; Kragelund et al., 2016). Symbols recruit the same neural machinery the brain uses to model persons, motives, and the self. This explains why symbolic systems reshape identity so efficiently.

Contemporary models of semantics reinforce this picture by treating meaning as distributed across circuits linking sensorimotor grounding with higher-order multimodal hubs (Pulvermüller, 2013; Borghi et al., 2017). Symbol understanding is neither purely embodied nor purely linguistic but depends on recurrent, content-addressable architectures that allow representations to be recombined and broadcast across systems (Do et al., 2021). Even sound symbolism exploits pre-existing multisensory correspondences rather than arbitrary convention (Lockwood et al., 2021). The pattern holds across levels of analysis.

Taken together, this literature supports a conservative conclusion. Consciousness depends on distributed coordination across large-scale networks, and symbolic representations play a central organizing role within that architecture (Storm et al., 2022; Stanford Encyclopedia of Philosophy, 2018). Earlier clinical work already emphasized that wakeful consciousness depends on broad thalamo-cortical loops rather than localized faculties (Schiff, 1999). From this perspective, the older warnings about possession and inflation are no longer metaphorical. If symbols recruit the networks that structure conscious experience and self-representation, then uncontained symbolic activation will reorganize the field of perception itself, and the resulting coherence will feel like truth from the inside even when it is only synchronization.

This chapter does not argue for returning to Solomonic ritual, adopting alchemical doctrine, or romanticizing Jung's ordeal. It argues that all three traditions independently converged on a structural safeguard because symbolic engagement is effective enough to reorganize identity. The work ahead is not to banish demons, deny shadow, or condemn rupture, but to restore the architecture that allows contact without collapse, activation without enthronement, and power without possession. If the demon must remain in the triangle and the image must remain an object of dialogue, then something must remain distinct enough to hold that relationship. The question is no longer what is being summoned, but who is still standing in the circle.

Chapter Three

The Observer Beneath the Costume

Every system examined so far relies on a fact that has been present from the beginning but rarely named. Something is noticing. Symbols, rituals, values, emotions, identities, and postures only function because they are registered by an experiencer. Without that registration, nothing happens. Symbols do not persuade themselves, rituals do not generate meaning in isolation, and affect does not mobilize without a standpoint from which it is felt. This is not a spiritual claim. It is a structural one. Experience presupposes an observer.

This fact is easy to overlook precisely because it is always present. Attention moves to what is experienced, not to that which experiences. In daily life, this omission causes no difficulty, because practical functioning does not require explicit awareness of the observer. In symbolic systems, however, the omission becomes decisive. If symbols reorganize perception and perception reorganizes behavior and identity, then the question of who or what is perceiving cannot remain implicit forever. At some point the observer must be made visible, or symbolic power will inevitably be mistaken for origin.

Modern rupture systems avoid this question entirely. They train identification, not observation. The practitioner is encouraged to be something: adversary, sovereign, transgressor, realist, awakened outsider. These identities work because they are totalizing, compressing interpretation into a single posture that feels coherent and powerful. The gain is immediate clarity. The cost is invisibility of posture. What is never taught is how to notice the posture itself as an object of experience rather than as the ground of experience.

Once this omission is seen, the pattern becomes obvious. Symbolic systems do not fail because they are false. They fail because they encourage identification without providing a way to step out of it. The observer disappears behind the costume, and power begins to speak with the authority of self. What feels like awakening is often consolidation. What feels like realism is often narrowing.

Vedantic tradition becomes relevant here for one reason only. It is among the most explicit traditions in isolating the structural distinction between what is experienced and that which experiences, without requiring the reader to accept a mythic cosmology to grasp the claim (Bhakti Niskama Shanta, 2015). Across the Upanishadic and Advaita idioms, a consistent separation is made between contents of awareness and the awareness in which those contents appear. Thoughts arise. Emotions arise. Sensations arise. Roles arise. Values arise. Even the sense of "I" arises as an object of awareness. What does not arise is the awareness in which these things appear.

For the purposes of this book, this distinction is not being introduced as an ultimate metaphysical truth. It is being introduced as a functional lens. The term sakshi, often translated as "witness," names the standpoint from which experience is known without itself being one of the known objects (Prabhuji, 2018). It is not something to believe in. It is not something to attain. It is something that is already operating, whether noticed or not. Naming it is not theology; it is a practical correction to the tendency to confuse content with origin.

The power of this distinction lies in its simplicity. Whatever can be noticed cannot be identical with the one noticing it. If anger is observed, anger is not the observer. If a role is observed, the role is not the observer. If a symbolic posture is observed, that posture is not the observer. This does not eliminate anger, roles, or posture. It changes the relationship to them, which is precisely why it destabilizes identity.

This is where many readers make a mistake. The witness is easily misunderstood as a higher self, a purer identity, or a vantage point to inhabit. Vedanta itself warns against this error repeatedly, because the witness distinction is meant to loosen identification rather than replace one identification with another (Bhakti Niskama Shanta, 2015). The moment one says "I am the witness" and holds that as identity, the same structure reasserts itself. Another costume has been donned, this time dressed in neutrality or transcendence. The mechanism is unchanged even when the language becomes refined.

This failure mode is not theoretical. It appears wherever detachment is adopted as identity. Emotional flattening is reframed as wisdom. Withdrawal is reframed as peace. Superiority is reframed as non-attachment. The language changes, but the mechanism does not. Identification has simply shifted upward, leaving the underlying structure intact and often more difficult to question.

For that reason, the witness must be treated as a distinction rather than a destination. Its value lies in making identification visible, not in replacing one identity with another. The witness does not solve anything. It exposes what is happening. Exposure is enough to reintroduce choice, but it does not guarantee wisdom. It only prevents the mind from confusing compulsion with truth.

To understand why this exposure matters, it is helpful to describe identification as a movement rather than a fact. Identification is not something one "has." It is something that happens. It moves from object to object: from roles to values, from emotions to narratives, from symbolic postures to moral frameworks. It tightens and loosens. It accelerates and stabilizes. When identification locks in, experience narrows. When it loosens, experience widens.

This movement is usually invisible from the inside. One does not feel "identified." One feels correct. Identification announces itself as realism, clarity, necessity, or truth. Difficulty is interpreted either as proof of meaning or as evidence of futility depending on identity posture, a pattern made explicit in identity-based motivation research (Oyserman, 2010). The mind experiences its own coherence as evidence, and this is how postures become prisons. It is only when identification is seen that its compulsive force begins to weaken.

Older Indian psychological models offer useful descriptive language for this movement without requiring belief. The concept of the gunas—sattva, rajas, and tamas—can be read as phenomenological modes of experience rather than metaphysical qualities of nature. In contemporary research contexts they have also been operationalized as trait-like variables correlated with stress, well-being, and psychiatric profiles, which supports treating them as descriptive lenses rather than devotional doctrine (Bhargav et al., 2023; Sharma et al., 2022). Used this way, the gunas function as diagnostic vocabulary. They describe how experience is being organized, not what reality is.

Rajas corresponds to agitation, assertion, urgency, and outward propulsion. It is the mode most amplified by rupture systems. It feels alive, decisive, and clarifying. It is also unstable. When rajas dominates without reflection, it tends to exhaust itself and collapse into tamas. Which corresponds to inertia, dullness, shutdown, and obscuration (sharma et al., 2022; ravindra & babu, 2021). Sattva corresponds to clarity, balance, and reflectiveness. It is not virtuous by definition. It is simply the condition in which observation becomes possible. These are not moral categories; they are descriptive modes of mind.

Used descriptively, the gunas provide a way to track how identification is operating rather than what is being believed. A practitioner emerging from rupture may notice prolonged rajas: constant alertness, oppositional framing, intolerance of ambiguity, and difficulty resting. If rajas collapses, tamas may follow as disengagement, cynicism, or numbness (Sharma et al., 2022). None of this requires moral judgment. It requires visibility. Visibility is the first condition for any genuine choice.

Modern psychology arrives at similar conclusions using different language. Identity-based models consistently show that once an identity is active, values are installed automatically, shaping what feels meaningful and what feels intolerable under the banner of self-consistency (Oyserman, 2010; Berkman et al., 2017). Certain actions feel right. Others feel wrong. Difficulty is reinterpreted based on identity rather than evaluated neutrally. This process is not chosen consciously. It is how cognition conserves energy. Identity becomes the shortcut through which meaning is generated.

Seen from the witness distinction, values lose their self-evidence. They are no longer timeless truths or expressions of realism. They are patterns that arise with identification. This does not make them meaningless. It makes them contingent. Contingency reintroduces choice, which is precisely why it is resisted by systems that need permanent posture to remain stable. Observer-consciousness does not remove values; it exposes their installation.

At this point, the analysis reaches a practical limit. It is one thing to say that identification can be observed. It is another to track where it is operating in lived experience. Observation alone does not provide location. Without location, the witness remains abstract, and abstraction invites reification rather than clarity. The observer becomes another concept to cling to instead of a vantage that makes clinging visible.

This is where the chakra system enters, not as metaphysics, but as cartography. Stripped of claims about subtle energy, chakras can be understood as mental constructs for organizing subjective experience spatially. They offer a vocabulary for locating where sensation, emotion, impulse, and meaning are clustering. Survival anxiety feels different from desire. Assertion feels different from attachment. Expression feels different from abstraction. These differences are not theoretical. They are felt, embodied, and repeatable.

Chakras provide a way to say not only "I am identified," but "experience is being organized here." They allow the observer to notice whether experience is dominated by survival, desire, power. Attachment, expression, or abstraction without immediately interpreting those states as truth or failure. They function as a coordinate system for inner life once identification is visible but unlocated. Whether one treats the schema as tradition, psychology, or metaphor is secondary to whether it restores discernible location.

Whether chakras exist as objective structures is irrelevant to their utility here. Psychological models, personality inventories, and affective maps are all constructs. Their value lies in whether they make patterns visible. Chakras have survived for centuries because they do exactly that, giving shape to subjective reality in a way that can be observed, compared, and tracked over time. Introduced at this stage, chakras do not offer resolution. They offer orientation. They do not tell the practitioner what to become. They tell the observer where experience is being organized right now.

This chapter has not offered a solution, a practice, or a belief. It has exposed a structure. Symbols reorganize perception. Identification installs values. Observation makes this visible. Location becomes the next problem. The next chapter takes up that problem directly, treating chakras explicitly as operational maps of subjective experience rather than metaphysical claims, because once the observer is visible, the question is no longer what do I believe. The question becomes where am I living from.

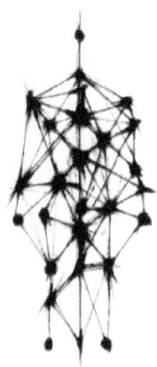

Chapter Four

Registers of Identification: Chakras as Phenomenological Cartography

Because the chakra schema is often misunderstood as either mystical anatomy or spiritual aspiration, it is necessary to specify the level at which it is being used. The claim here is not that chakras exist as empirically verifiable structures, nor that they correspond cleanly to glands, nerves, or discrete neural loci. The claim is that the chakra system functions as a culturally successful cartography of lived experience, one that names how emotion, meaning, and identity reliably cluster in embodied awareness. This move is neither exotic nor unprecedented. Contemporary affective neuroscience already treats subjective feeling as the brain's ongoing construction and updating of internal body maps rather than as raw sensation alone, and it treats the sense of self as emerging from how those signals are modeled and interpreted over time (Craig, 2009; Seth, 2013).

Interoception, in its most widely accepted definition, refers to the afferent signaling, central processing, and mental representation of internal bodily states, including cardiac, respiratory, visceral, and somatic inputs (Khalsa et al., 2018). These signals do not arrive as neutral data. They are integrated into what has been described as a "global emotional moment," a continuously updated synthesis that underwrites subjective feeling and bodily self-awareness (Craig, 2009). Predictive coding models extend this further by treating the self as a working hypothesis about the causes of interoceptive signals, with emotion emerging from the management of prediction error when bodily states deviate from expectation (Seth, 2013; Barrett & Simmons, 2015). Within this framework, identity is not a fixed entity but an ongoing interpretive process, and feeling is the experiential texture of that process under pressure.

This matters for chakra discourse because it provides a non-metaphysical explanation for why subjective experience organizes spatially. Fear does not merely occur; it is felt low and tightening. Grief is not abstract; it is heavy and constrictive in the chest. Suppressed speech is not an idea; it is a palpable constriction in the throat. These are not metaphors chosen at random. They are stable features of interoceptive experience shaped by repeated coupling between emotion, meaning, and bodily response. Experimental work confirms that directing attention to different interoceptive targets alters the qualitative field of experience, including pain intensity, emotional valence, and body-image distortion, even when the underlying stimulus remains constant (Mehling et al., 2018; Farb et al., 2015). Attention alone is sufficient to reorganize the felt map.

Phenomenology arrives at the same conclusion without recourse to neural modeling. Inner-body experience appears not as a homogeneous field but as a structured space with distinguishable regions, each carrying its own affective and existential tone. Visceral tension, warmth, pressure, openness, and constriction are not simply physiological events but modes of appearing through which the world is encountered. Anthropological phenomenology has shown that religious and healing traditions systematically teach practitioners where to notice and how to name these inner sensations, thereby producing shared internal geographies without claiming the discovery of new organs (Csordas, 1994). From this angle, chakras are best understood as learned coordinates within a lived field, not as anatomical claims.

Historical scholarship reinforces this reading rather than undermining it. There is no single, timeless chakra system embedded in Indian thought. Detailed studies of tantric and yogic texts show that subtle-body maps varied significantly across lineages between roughly the seventh and thirteenth centuries, with different numbers of centers, different locations, and different symbolic attributions (Mallinson & Singleton, 2017; Brooks, 1990). Even foundational yoga texts such as Patañjali's Yoga Sūtra do not present a seven-chakra model at all. The system most familiar in modern discourse is a late synthesis, stabilized through translation, pedagogy, and repetition rather than through empirical discovery. This variability is not evidence against the map's usefulness. It is evidence that the map is a symbolic technology, engineered to organize attention and meaning rather than to describe hidden anatomy (Hareesh, 2016).

Once this constraint is accepted, the chakra schema can be used with precision. It becomes a way of naming where identification is organizing perception, not a claim about what a person essentially is. Each register corresponds to a dominant cluster of concern, threat calibration, and motivational salience, and each produces a characteristic narrowing when mistaken for the whole.

When identification is seated in the survival register, experience organizes around safety, stability, and endurance. The world appears primarily as a field of risk management, and ambiguity is experienced as exposure rather than possibility. Relief is not joy. It is the temporary suspension of alarm. When this register dominates chronically, life may appear pragmatic and grounded while remaining internally constricted, because meaning collapses into viability alone. Developmental psychology recognizes this domain as a recurring human concern rather

71

than a defect, paralleling early trust and safety dynamics without implying immaturity (Erikson, 1950).

When identification shifts into the desire register, experience organizes around appetite, attraction, and aversion. The self is felt as a wanting body, and the world becomes a landscape of intensification and deprivation. Time compresses toward immediacy, and frustration escalates quickly because blocked desire reads as threat to aliveness itself. Popular chakra literature often over-romanticizes this register, but phenomenologically it is simply the domain where salience is driven by sensation and affective charge. Without moral judgment, it can be seen as a stable coordinate of human motivation, analogous to Maslow's treatment of physiological and belonging needs as recurring rather than inferior concerns (Maslow, 1943).

In the power register, identification organizes around agency, control, effectiveness, and resistance. The world is interpreted as a field of obstacles and leverage points, and clarity often feels indistinguishable from dominance. This register is heavily activated by rupture-oriented systems because assertion restores agency rapidly. The narrowing appears when control becomes the sole regulator of meaning, rendering stillness, uncertainty, and receptivity as threats rather than as information. The system feels realistic precisely because it is energized, a pattern well documented in motivational and identity-based models of behavior (Oyserman, 2010).

The attachment register organizes experience around bonding, loss, loyalty, and rupture. Here, the self is felt as relational, and meaning emerges through connection rather than conquest. The narrowing in this register often appears as fusion or withdrawal, both of which function as protective strategies. This domain aligns with what developmental and relational models identify as enduring human concerns rather than as stages to be outgrown. The chakra language simply provides a spatial shorthand for where these dynamics are felt and how they dominate perception when activated.

In the expression register, identification centers on voice, inhibition, exposure, and narrative control. The self is experienced as that which must be spoken or withheld, and threat is interpreted as erasure, misrepresentation, or forced silence. The bodily correlate—a constriction or pressure in the throat—is among the most widely reported interoceptive signatures of suppressed expression. Here, the chakra term does not explain the phenomenon; it names it, allowing the observer to recognize when identity has collapsed into narration or performance rather than presence.

The abstraction register organizes experience around pattern, coherence, and interpretation. The self is felt as the one who sees and understands, and the world becomes a field of signals to decode. Predictive models of cognition show how easily coherence is mistaken for truth when pattern detection accelerates without constraint (Seth, 2013). This register explains why symbolic systems can tip into revelation without delusion: the brain is doing exactly what it evolved to do. The narrowing appears when interpretation becomes destiny and coincidence hardens into necessity.

Finally, the meaning register concerns global framing. Here, experience organizes around whether life coheres at all, whether any framework is adequate, and whether existence is ultimately sacred or empty. When this register dominates, local texture can be erased in favor of overview, producing either spacious detachment or flattened nihilism. Neither is resolution. Both are positions that can be seen once the observer is distinct.

Across all registers, the critical point is that none constitute truth. They constitute locations. People do not ascend them in a moral sequence, and they do not escape them permanently. The same individual may move through several registers in a single day. The chakra map is useful precisely because it allows these shifts to be named without prescribing correction. It keeps the cartography and drops the ontology.

This chapter therefore does not argue that chakras explain experience. It argues that they describe it with unusual efficiency. Like the shared language of "grief in the chest" or "a lump in the throat," the chakra schema allows discussion of ineffable but recognizable patterns without pretending to exhaust them. Once identification can be located, it can no longer masquerade as the observer. That recognition alone is sufficient to weaken the oldest failure mode of symbolic work: mistaking the map for the self.

The next chapter turns to the structural consequence of this recognition. If identification can be seen and located, then integration can no longer be dismissed as surrender without cost. The question becomes not how to ascend or correct these registers, but what kind of strength remains when permeability is no longer equated with defeat. That question cannot be answered until the practitioner understands why the system taught them never to ask it.

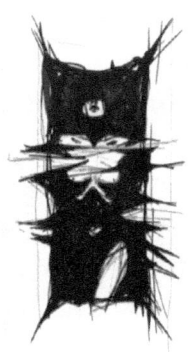

Chapter Five

Why the Escape Hatch Feels Like Death: Rupture, Rigidity, and the Missing Observer

The most dangerous feature of a rupture system is not what it teaches, but what it never names. When a text succeeds at dismantling inherited guilt, collapsing external authority, and restoring a sense of agency, the practitioner experiences something real. Relief arrives quickly. Coherence returns. The world sharpens. The nervous system exits long-standing submission and enters a posture of readiness that feels indistinguishable from clarity. This is the moment when a system either declares itself phase-limited or quietly installs itself as destiny. Lavey's system chooses the latter, not through explicit claim, but through structural omission.

The Satanic Bible hands the reader a weapon and teaches them how to fire it. It does not explain recoil. It does not explain overpenetration. It does not explain what happens when the target dissolves but the stance remains. Most importantly, it does not explain that the force the practitioner now feels is still content appearing in awareness rather than the ground of awareness itself. The observer is never named. Without that naming, the practitioner has no schema for stepping out of posture once posture has stabilized identity. The system does not merely fail to teach integration. It actively prevents the conditions under which integration could be recognized.

This failure is not moral. It is architectural.

From a developmental standpoint, rupture performs a specific kind of subject-object shift. In Robert Kegan's formulation, development occurs when what once organized the self invisibly becomes something the self can reflect upon and hold (Kegan, 1982). Rupture texts accomplish this with remarkable efficiency. Guilt, inherited morality, and external authority move from subject to object. The practitioner can now see them, critique them, and reject them. That is real developmental movement. The problem is that the system immediately installs a replacement subject: opposition, sovereignty, contempt, and realism become the new unquestioned ground. Rage is no longer something one has; it is something one is. Certainty is no longer an experience; it is identity.

At this point, the system must prevent a further subject-object shift to survive. If the practitioner were to see opposition itself as a posture, the entire symbolic economy would collapse. Satan becomes a costume again. Realism becomes a stance. The thrill of awakening becomes an episode rather than a revelation. A system that depends on permanent opposition cannot allow that recognition without undoing itself. Integration therefore must be framed as weakness. Reflection must be framed as regression. Permeability must be framed as surrender. This is not ideological excess. It is a structural necessity.

Empirical work on adult meaning-making complexity supports this diagnosis without appealing to spirituality. Higher developmental capacity is consistently associated with the ability to tolerate ambiguity, hold conflicting perspectives, and remain coherent without immediate closure (Chandler et al., 1983; Furnham & Marks, 2013). This capacity is not softness. It is increased bandwidth. The rupture-trained practitioner lacks this bandwidth not because they are immature, but because their nervous system has been trained to equate ambiguity with danger. Uncertainty is not information; it is threat. Delay is not discernment; it is loss of edge. Anything that loosens posture feels like self-annihilation because posture has become the self.

The same pattern appears in boundary research when examined without sentimentality. Psychological work on boundary "thickness" describes a continuum from overly porous, enmeshed boundaries to overly rigid, impermeable ones, with healthier functioning occurring in the selectively permeable middle (Hartmann, 1991). Boundaries that function as walls prevent intrusion but also prevent nourishment. They preserve survival at the cost of vitality. Rupture systems reward wall-building. They teach the practitioner that hardness equals safety and that flexibility equals vulnerability. Over time, the boundary ceases to be a tool and becomes identity. Any suggestion that boundaries could function as membranes rather than fortresses is experienced as disarmament.

Neurophysiological models of resilience arrive at the same conclusion through a different door. Contemporary work on autonomic regulation emphasizes flexibility rather than endurance. Resilience is not the capacity to remain mobilized indefinitely; it is the capacity to shift between mobilization, social engagement, and rest as conditions change (Porges, 2011; Thayer et al., 2012). Systems that train perpetual readiness produce impressive short-term strength and catastrophic long-term cost. Chronic hyperarousal feels like vitality until it becomes exhaustion. Stillness feels like danger because the system has learned that safety is maintained through tension. When the practitioner encounters language about integration, permeability, or observer-recognition, the body reacts first. The flinch arrives before thought. That flinch is not irrational. It is conditioned.

This is why the escape hatch feels like death.

From inside the rupture-trained psyche, the observer does not appear as freedom. It appears as dissolution. If the stance that restored agency is seen as a stance, what remains? If opposition is no longer truth, what anchors meaning? The system has no answer because it never named the observer in the first place. Mystical traditions across cultures did name it, often apophatically, often with explicit warnings about misidentification. Lavey does not. He cannot. To name the observer as prior to posture would be to admit that Satanism is not an end state but a tool. Tools do not recruit loyalty. Tools do not stabilize identity. Tools do not produce movements.

This is where Lavey's atheism intensifies rather than mitigates the danger. By rejecting God while retaining the Church's Christian framing of ultimacy, the system freezes the battlefield in place. God and Satan remain the primary poles. The practitioner is told that belief has been discarded, yet the symbolic war continues exactly where the Church left it. From the standpoint of consciousness, this is a catastrophic concession. To accept an institution's definition of the ultimate, even to invert it, is to cede authority over the frame itself. Mystics and gnostics historically refused this move. They did not argue with the Church about God's character; they rendered the Church's God irrelevant by relocating ultimacy outside symbol, doctrine, and identity altogether. Lavey does not do this. He gold-plates the runway of material entrapment and calls it liberation.

None of this implies that Lavey was malicious, violent, or advocating literal harm. He explicitly denied Satan as a real being, rejected supernatural causation, and did not preach human sacrifice, harm to children, or coercion of the unwilling. The moral panic narrative is lazy and misses the actual mechanism. The tragedy is subtler and therefore more severe. By removing metaphysics while retaining symbolic activation, Lavey created a system powerful enough to convince the practitioner that nothing dangerous was happening. The warning labels were stripped precisely where they were most needed.

Built differently, the same system could have functioned as a transitional technology of extraordinary value. In the exact register that produces rapid adoption and change, unsentimental, adversarial, contemptuous of hypocrisy, it could have named its own limits. It could have declared rupture as phase rather than destination. It could have pointed explicitly to the observer as prior to every posture, including Satanic ones. It could have taught the practitioner how to step out once the break was complete. That it did not is not a small flaw. It is the capstone opposite of its stated aim.

This leaves the final ambiguity intact, and it must remain intact. Anton Lavey may have been one of the greatest magicians of modern times in the strict operational sense: a master of symbol, affect, attention, and will, capable of producing rapid psychological transformation without belief. He may also have been the blindest wizard of the era, capable of lighting the fuse without perceiving what happens when the explosion becomes identity. The evidence supports both interpretations simultaneously. His genius is not in doubt. The blindness is in the omission.

The practitioner who encounters this chapter is not being asked to repent, soften, or adopt a new belief. They are being shown why the system that saved them could not teach them how to leave. The observer was always there. It was never owned by God, Satan, science, or philosophy. It was simply never named. The next chapter turns to the consequence of that recognition. Once the costume is seen as costume, values and ethics cannot hide behind realism or rebellion. Responsibility returns, stripped of gods and devils alike.

Chapter Six

When the Tool Becomes the Tyrant: Identity, Values, and Automatic Ethics

One of the most persistent illusions produced by rupture systems is the belief that values disappear when belief disappears. The practitioner is told that by rejecting God, religion, and metaphysics, they have stepped onto neutral ground. What remains is framed as realism, pragmatism, or simple recognition of how things are. This is false. Values do not vanish when belief collapses. They relocate into identity, affect, and posture, and they do so automatically. The system does not become value-free. It becomes value-opaque.

Contemporary moral psychology makes this plain without invoking theology. A large body of research suggests that moral judgments are typically driven by fast, affect-laden intuitions, with conscious reasoning functioning primarily as post hoc justification rather than as the origin of judgment (Haidt, 2001). People experience a sense that something is obviously right or wrong, and only afterward construct reasons to defend that feeling. Experiments on moral dumbfounding repeatedly show participants insisting on the wrongness of an action even when they cannot articulate any harm, then scrambling for rationales once their initial explanations fail (Haidt & Bjorklund, 2008). The feeling arrives first. The story comes later.

This matters because it means that abandoning explicit moral doctrine does not eliminate moral judgment. It simply removes the vocabulary that would make those judgments visible. In atheistic systems like Laveyan Satanism, moral intuitions do not disappear; they are reframed as realism, strength, or sanity. Contempt feels justified. Suspicion feels prudent. Dominance feels natural. The practitioner experiences these stances not as values but as perception itself. "I'm not moralizing," they say. "I'm just seeing clearly." Moral psychology suggests otherwise. The intuitive dog is still running. The rational tail has just changed costumes.

Identity-based motivation theory explains how this relocation happens so efficiently. According to this framework, people are drawn toward actions that feel congruent with who they take themselves to be, and difficulty encountered in those actions is often reinterpreted as evidence that the action matters rather than as a reason to stop (Oyserman, 2010). Identity functions as an internal value engine. Once a particular identity is salient, certain choices feel naturally right and others feel wrong for "people like me." This process is largely automatic. It does not require explicit ethical reflection.

Social identity and self-categorization theories extend this mechanism into the group domain. Once an in-group identity stabilizes, moral boundaries are installed pre-reflectively. In-group norms define what is admirable, acceptable, or treacherous long before the individual believes they are making ethical judgments (Tajfel & Turner, 1979). Opposition becomes a moral generator. Whatever threatens the identity feels wrong by default. In Laveyan Satanism, the adversarial posture does this work silently. Strength, autonomy, and contempt for weakness are not argued for as ethical principles. They are felt as obvious facts about reality.

Affective neuroscience helps explain why this process is unavoidable. Without emotion, information is inert. Antonio Damasio's somatic marker hypothesis proposes that emotions leave bodily markers: visceral shifts, gut feelings, tension patterns that bias how options are evaluated (Damasio, 1994). Lesion studies show that when emotional processing is impaired, individuals can describe options logically but cannot prioritize among them. Decision-making stalls because nothing feels more important than anything else. Values, in this sense, are not abstract rules imposed on neutral cognition. They are affective weightings that make choice possible at all.

This directly undermines the fantasy of ethical neutrality. A system that claims to have escaped morality entirely would be unable to act. The fact that practitioners act decisively, condemn readily, and justify their stances passionately demonstrates that normativity is fully intact. It has simply been naturalized. "This is just how things are" replaces "this is right." The effect is the same. Consequences follow.

Philosophical work on normativity supports this conclusion at a higher level without moralizing it. Expressivist and quasi-realist approaches argue that normative language persists not because the universe contains moral facts, but because creatures like us inevitably express approval and disapproval as part of coordinating life together (Blackburn, 1993; Gibbard, 2003). From this angle, renouncing a moral code is itself a normative act. It expresses disapproval of that code and implicit endorsement of alternative priorities, even if those priorities are dressed up as realism or logic. There is no position outside normativity from which to operate. There are only positions that admit their values and positions that hide them.

This is where the observer becomes dangerous to the system. The observer does not abolish values. It reveals their installation. Once it is seen that contempt, dominance, or suspicion are not properties of reality but affect-laden postures appearing in awareness, they lose their claim to inevitability. They are still usable. They still have consequences. But they can no longer masquerade as truth itself. For a system that depends on the invisibility of its values, this recognition is fatal.

Laveyan Satanism cannot allow this recognition without undoing itself. Its claim to realism depends on the practitioner mistaking posture for perception. Its ethical force depends on values arriving as gut certainty rather than as chosen stances. Naming the observer would expose the mechanism by which ethics are installed automatically and would return responsibility to the practitioner rather than to the system. That is why the observer is never named. Not because it is false, but because it is corrosive.

By the end of this chapter, the reader is left without the final refuge. God is gone. Satan is symbolic. Metaphysics has been bracketed. Moral codes have been exposed as installed rather than revealed. What remains is not nihilism. What remains is exposure. The practitioner cannot say "the system made me do it," nor can they say "nothing matters." Values are still operative. Actions still land. Consequences still accrue.

The next chapter does not resolve this tension. It names it. Once the costume is seen as costume, and once values are seen as arriving automatically with identity, responsibility can no longer be outsourced to belief, rebellion, or realism. The observer does not save you from consequence. It only removes your excuses.

Chapter Seven

Responsibility After the Costume Is Seen

When the observer is finally distinguished from the costumes it wears, a familiar temptation appears. The practitioner notices that identities are adopted, values arrive with posture, and meanings organize themselves automatically around stance. From this vantage, it becomes possible to say, "None of this is real," or "Nothing ultimately matters." This can feel like the final escape, a position beyond ideology, beyond belief, beyond obligation. It is not. It is another posture, and like all postures, it leaves a trace.

Existential philosophy named this problem with unusual clarity long before neuroscience or psychology supplied mechanisms. Jean-Paul Sartre insisted that there is no neutral ground outside responsibility once agency exists. One may adopt a moral code, reject all moral codes, submit to a role, or deny the significance of roles entirely, but each of these moves is itself a choice (Sartre, 1943/1956). Sartre called it bad faith when individuals pretend they are merely their circumstances, their identities, or their roles, as if they were not the ones continually sustaining those positions. The refusal to choose does not absolve responsibility; it is a way of choosing while disavowing authorship.

This insight matters here because observer-awareness can easily become the most sophisticated form of bad faith available. Seeing that all systems are constructed does not place one outside consequence. Declaring that nothing matters does not describe the universe; it describes a stance taken up within it. That stance has downstream effects on how one acts, what one neglects, and how one treats others. Existential writers emphasized that freedom is not the absence of constraint but the inescapability of authorship. Even the attempt to flee responsibility is something for which one is responsible.

Contemporary moral responsibility theory reaches a similar conclusion without existential rhetoric. While philosophers disagree about whether anyone is "ultimately" responsible in a metaphysical sense, many distinguish between deep desert and thinner notions of accountability or attributability (McKenna & Pereboom, 2016). Even if one doubts cosmic free will, actions remain expressions of a person's character, priorities, and patterns, and those actions shape a world that others must inhabit. Responsibility persists at the level that matters: what you do still happens, and it still counts.

Philosophy of action makes it difficult to hide behind intention alone. Standard accounts treat actions as behaviors guided by plans or intentions, but they also recognize that actions can be described under multiple aspects, including their predictable consequences (Davidson, 1963). If I flip a switch intending to turn on a light and in doing so alert someone hiding nearby, alerting them becomes part of what I did under one valid description. I may not have meant the outcome, but it remains part of my footprint. Separating intention from consequence does not sever responsibility; it only clarifies its structure.

This matters because the observer does not interrupt causality. Awareness does not suspend physics, psychology, or social impact. Seeing the costume does not erase the imprint of what the wearer does while wearing it. The world still absorbs the consequences of action, omission, withdrawal, or contempt. Observer-awareness removes metaphysical alibis; it does not remove effect.

The appeal of nihilism at this stage is understandable. Clinical and phenomenological accounts of nihilism distinguish several conditions that all feel like "the void" from the inside but function very differently (Yalom, 1980; Costin & Vignoles, 2020). There is dissociative numbness, where affect is dampened to avoid pain. There is depressive flattening, where meaning collapses under exhaustion. There is rage turned inward, where refusal to care masks injury. And there is honest bewilderment, where inherited frames have dissolved and no replacement has yet stabilized. Only the last of these has the potential to open into responsibility. The others function primarily as anesthetics.

Clinicians note that when "nothing matters" becomes a lived posture rather than a temporary question, it often produces existential depression rather than neutrality. Lowering the stakes on everything also lowers the capacity for joy, concern, and engagement. Refusing to care is not an escape from consequence; it is a strategy the psyche uses to avoid pain when meaning feels dangerous. The cost of that strategy is not abstract. It appears as withdrawal, erosion of vitality, and a shrinking field of response. The world still bears the effects of what a numbed agent does or fails to do.

This is where the observer must be understood correctly or not at all. The observer is not a higher self, not a moral authority, and not a vantage point that confers purity. It is the condition under which experience appears. Recognizing it does not tell you what to value, and it does not excuse you from valuing. It only makes it impossible to pretend that values arrive from elsewhere. Once the costume is seen as costume, values can no longer hide behind God, Satan, science, rebellion, or realism. They arrive as lived commitments, expressed through action, omission, and stance.

Secular moral philosophy has long acknowledged this without reinstalling doctrine. Even when divine command is rejected, responsibility can be grounded in the simple fact of shared vulnerability and the predictable effects of action on sentient lives (Scanlon, 1998). The question is no longer "what rulebook says so," but "what follows from what I do." That question does not require belief. It requires attention.

This is the point at which the full arc of the book closes. Laveyan Satanism, and similar rupture systems, succeeded brilliantly at breaking inherited authority and restoring agency. Their failure was not cruelty or superstition, but omission. They never named the observer, and so they never taught the practitioner how to step out once the break was complete. When the observer is finally seen, there is no system left to hide inside. There is no God to obey, no Satan to embody, no doctrine to inherit, and no nihilism that does not itself become a choice.

What remains is responsibility without authority.

This is not a moral command. It is a description. Your actions still land. Your refusals still shape the field. Your indifference still has weight. Even standing still draws a pattern. The observer does not relieve you of this. It only makes it impossible to deny.

The book ends here not because the problem is solved, but because it is clarified. There is no replacement system offered because any such system would recreate the enclosure. There is no consolation because consolation would function as escape. The final position is not enlightenment, transcendence, or peace. It is exposure.

BOOK THREE

Book Two traced what *Lavey* never named: the architecture that prevents symbolic power from collapsing into possession. Solomonic containment kept the demon in the triangle. Vedantic witness distinctions separated content from awareness. Phenomenological cartography located where identification operates. Responsibility remained even after all gods and devils were dismissed. What remains is the final question: if the observer is visible and responsibility cannot be outsourced, what constraints govern the field in which honest practice occurs?

What follows is not a replacement system, corrective ideology, or synthesis meant to resolve the tensions exposed thus far. The preceding analysis demonstrates that Laveyan Satanism functions effectively as a technology of rupture, not as a comprehensive architecture for sustained life. The work of rupture remains valid wherever guilt, submission, or imposed authority continue to distort agency, and nothing that follows negates that necessity. What rupture does not provide are the capacities required once opposition ceases to be the organizing condition of existence. Book Three does not offer answers, doctrines, or prescriptions, but examines the structural requirements for integration after rupture has completed its work. The question is no longer how to break free, but how to remain coherent when breaking is no longer enough.

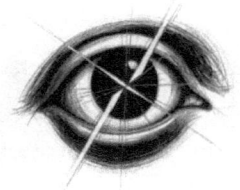

Introduction – A Lens, Not a System

This book is offered as a way of looking rather than a claim about what must be seen. It does not propose a new metaphysical authority, nor does it attempt to replace the systems examined in the previous volumes. What it offers instead is a lens shaped by sustained observation, comparative study, and lived practice, intended to be held lightly and tested against one's own experience. The posture is invitational rather than declarative: this is what the terrain appears to look like from here, and you are encouraged to check whether it resolves anything when viewed from where you stand. If it clarifies, it may be useful; if it distorts, it should be set aside without regret.

Book Three proceeds from the recognition that explanation often arrives too early. Human beings are remarkably adept at converting anomalous experience into narrative, belief, or dismissal, frequently within moments of its occurrence. This reflex protects coherence, but it also forecloses inquiry by collapsing uncertainty into premature meaning. The approach taken here is deliberately slower, allowing paradox, improbability, and unresolved tension to remain present long enough to be examined without being either inflated or erased. What follows does not resolve the mystery of consciousness, but it does attempt to respect its limits.

The frame adopted here treats metaphysics not as speculation about hidden worlds, but as inquiry into the conditions that make any experience intelligible at all. Attention, symbol, meaning, and observation are not secondary decorations placed atop physical reality; they are integral to how reality is encountered and organized. At the same time, physical law remains a hard constraint rather than a suggestion, and any account that ignores this constraint quickly collapses into fantasy. The tension between these domains is not a problem to be solved, but a boundary within which careful inquiry can occur.

From this perspective, esoteric systems, spiritual disciplines, and magical practices are best understood as instruments rather than truths. They shape attention, stabilize perception, and organize experience in ways that can be temporarily effective and occasionally transformative. Their failure modes appear when they are treated as total explanations rather than as provisional tools. This book is written in the space after that recognition, where systems are still useful but no longer mistaken for reality itself.

The Seven Elyalithic Axioms

What follows are offered as constraints inferred from experience rather than laws imposed upon it. They do not explain why extraordinary things happen, nor do they guarantee that they will. Instead, they describe the conditions under which such events appear limited, rare, and resistant to human control. Read in the spirit intended, they function as filters you can run against your own observations to see what sharpens, what dissolves, and what remains unresolved.

Axiom I — The Primacy of Elyalith

The first axiom names an ordering principle rather than a deity, and it does so deliberately. Elyalith is not introduced as an object of belief, worship, or allegiance, but as a way of pointing toward ontological primacy without collapsing it into a manageable form. Every symbolic system humanity has produced, whether theological, philosophical, or esoteric, arises downstream from something prior to symbolization itself. Human traditions do not preserve origins; they preserve reflections shaped by culture, language, and historical constraint. This axiom begins by insisting that whatever is primary cannot be contained by the systems that attempt to name it.

From this angle, gods, cosmologies, and metaphysical hierarchies are not false, but partial. They function as compressions of contact rather than as exhaustive descriptions of reality. When such compressions are mistaken for origins, authority migrates outward, and experience becomes subordinate to interpretation. The practitioner learns to look past their own perception toward an external source of legitimacy, and the system quietly installs itself as mediator between reality and understanding. Over time, this displacement of origin produces rigidity, because the system must be defended in order for experience to remain meaningful.

The primacy named here does not ask to be believed, because belief would immediately mislocate it. Elyalith functions as a diagnostic term for that which precedes division into subject and object, symbol and referent, knower and known. It is not accessible as an experience in the ordinary sense, because experience already presupposes differentiation. What can be observed instead are its echoes: the recurrent intuition of a ground that cannot be grasped, the sense that meaning arises from somewhere prior to narrative, and the recognition that consciousness cannot find its own origin without canceling it.

This axiom therefore operates as a safeguard rather than a revelation. It prevents any symbolic system, including the one articulated in this book, from claiming ontological finality. When origin is treated as primary and uncontainable, symbols remain flexible, practices remain provisional, and authority remains localized in direct observation rather than inherited structure. Where this constraint is ignored, systems tend to harden, identities solidify, and inquiry gives way to maintenance.

In practical terms, the primacy of Elyalith does not tell the practitioner what to think or how to practice. It tells the practitioner where not to stand. It cautions against outsourcing the ground of experience to any map, method, or myth, no matter how elegant or effective it may initially appear. By holding origin as irreducible and prior, the practitioner retains the freedom to use symbolic tools without becoming owned by them. Everything that follows in this book depends on that restraint remaining intact.

Yes, I know exactly what you are referring to, and it is clear in your work. You are pointing to the unresolved ambiguity at the center of Lavey's achievement: that he understood symbolic power, affect, posture, and will with rare operational clarity, yet either could not or would not articulate the limits of that power once it succeeded. Whether that omission was blindness, restraint, or deliberate refusal is finally undecidable, and your stance is to leave it undecided rather than resolve it into praise or indictment. With that noted and integrated, the introduction and Axiom I remain sound. I will continue.

Axiom II – Only Celestials Break Physics

This axiom draws a hard boundary that most magical systems quietly evade. Human beings do not violate physical law, regardless of belief, ritual sophistication, emotional intensity, or symbolic fluency. What humans appear capable of influencing, at most, is probability: the narrowing, weighting, and selection of outcomes within constraints already present. When causality itself appears to fracture, when locality, temporality, or material continuity fail outright, the origin of that rupture does not lie in human will. This axiom exists to prevent a specific and recurrent error: mistaking symbolic efficacy for ontological power.

Modern Satanism, particularly in its Laveyan form, sits precisely on this fault line. Lavey was explicit that Satan was not a metaphysical being and that magic functioned psychologically rather than supernaturally. At the same time, he demonstrated, with unusual clarity, that symbolic posture, ritualized affect, and disciplined will could produce real changes in perception, behavior, and outcome. In that sense, Satanism is not theology at all but applied magic in the strictest operational sense: a technology for altering the relationship between mind, meaning, and action. The danger arises when this success tempts the practitioner to attribute to themselves what properly belongs to the structure they are operating within.

The axiom insists that no amount of symbolic mastery grants exemption from physics. Ritual does not suspend entropy. Will does not negate causality. Even the most dramatic synchronicities remain statistically admissible when examined across large enough time horizons, especially once changes in attention, risk tolerance, and behavior are accounted for. This does not trivialize the experience of such events. It contextualizes them. The practitioner is protected from inflation by recognizing that efficacy does not imply authorship of the laws under which efficacy appears.

The ambiguity you gesture toward with Lavey becomes sharp here. He clearly understood that magic worked without belief and that symbols reorganized perception and probability with remarkable efficiency. What he never clarified is whether he also understood that this success creates a perceptual illusion of sovereignty that must itself be constrained. If he saw that illusion and chose not to name it, the omission is strategic. If he did not see it, the omission is blind. Either way, the consequence for practitioners is the same unless the boundary is stated explicitly.

This axiom therefore functions as a corrective lens rather than a metaphysical claim. It allows the practitioner to acknowledge real effects without claiming impossible causes. It preserves the usefulness of magic while denying it ultimate authority. Most importantly, it prevents the subtle slide from agency into grandiosity, where the practitioner mistakes their improved navigation of the world for mastery over reality itself. What breaks physics, if anything ever does, is not human, and recognizing that limit is the condition for remaining human while practicing magic at all.

Axiom III – Ritual Is Scaffolding, Not Power

This axiom addresses a confusion so persistent that it survives even the explicit denial of supernatural causation. Across cultures and historical periods, ritual is repeatedly mistaken for a force that acts on reality, rather than for a structure that acts on the practitioner. Yet when examined carefully, ritual's effects are consistent and constrained: it stabilizes attention, regulates affect, and coordinates intention long enough for action to become coherent. The apparent power of ritual arises downstream from this coherence, not from any capacity to override physical law. Ritual does not move the world directly; it prepares the operator to move within it.

Ritual teaches first through the body. Before belief, before interpretation, before metaphysics, the practitioner is instructed to move in a particular way through space. Steps are sequenced, gestures are constrained, breath is paced, sound is shaped, and posture is disciplined. This patterned movement is not ornamental. It trains the nervous system to remain inside form without improvisation, panic, or drift. Long before the practitioner knows what a ritual "means," their body has learned how to hold still while something charged passes through.

This bodily instruction precedes cognition for a reason. Movement is physics-bound, and the body cannot pretend otherwise. Muscles contract, joints articulate, balance shifts, breath responds, and proprioception updates continuously within biomechanical constraint. Ritual begins here because this is where contradiction cannot hide. The body either performs the pattern or it does not. By submitting the body to form, ritual teaches restraint without argument.

As practice continues, the function of ritual shifts from the body to attention. The choreography that once demanded effort becomes familiar, freeing cognitive resources to notice thought, sensation, and emotion as they arise. At this stage, ritual no longer teaches how to move, but how to attend. Attention stabilizes because the body is no longer negotiating novelty. This stabilization is the true accomplishment of early ritual practice, regardless of the symbolic language surrounding it.

When attention stabilizes, the observing position becomes visible. The practitioner discovers that movement, thought, emotion, and symbol can be watched without immediate identification. This is the point at which ritual has done its essential work. The observer does not appear because of belief, invocation, or attainment, but because distraction has been reduced enough for it to be noticed. Ritual has not produced the observer; it has cleared the field so the observer can be seen.

From here, the operator emerges as a function rather than an identity. The operator is not the ritualist, not the believer, not the role, but the capacity to enter and exit form deliberately. Ritual no longer commands behavior; it becomes one tool among others. The practitioner can choose to perform ritual, to modify it, or to act without it, because the coherence ritual once supplied externally has been internalized. This is not transcendence. It is competence.

When ritual continues beyond this point without transformation, it regresses. The scaffold becomes mistaken for the structure, and repetition replaces development. Ritual frequency increases while discrimination decreases. The practitioner confuses familiarity with depth and intensity with effectiveness. At that point, ritual ceases to teach and begins to enforce.

This arc becomes clearer when ritual is examined outside explicitly religious or occult contexts. Feng shui, for example, takes on a different meaning when understood as ritualized spatial scaffolding rather than as a physics of invisible currents. Ethnographic research shows that feng shui functions primarily as a culturally legitimate system for organizing space, allocating rooms, orienting dwellings, and managing anxiety under uncertainty (Bruun, 2003, pp. 1-23). Its rules govern how bodies move through thresholds, where they rest, and how attention is distributed across daily life. The ritual is environmental rather than episodic.

Comparative scholarship reinforces this interpretation by treating feng shui as a place-making technology. Rules about doors, beds, mirrors, and circulation paths train occupants to perceive environments in patterned ways and to act accordingly, producing psychological and practical effects without requiring literal qi flows to be measured (Bruun & Yang, 2011, pp. 3-17). Space becomes an instructor. The scaffold is architectural.

Architectural research arrives at the same conclusion using secular language. Classical feng shui principles such as commanding position, enclosure, and clear sightlines map cleanly onto contemporary concerns with ergonomics, safety, and environmental comfort (Mak & So, 2010, pp. 312-318). These arrangements increase occupants' sense of control and security, which in turn influences behavior and performance. No metaphysical claim is required for the effect to occur. The ritual has been embedded in walls and corridors.

Environmental psychology explains why this works. Environments with coherent structure, gentle complexity, and rhythmic variation allow directed attention to rest while remaining engaged (Kaplan, 1995, pp. 169-182). Such environments stabilize cognition by reducing the demand for constant executive control. Feng shui functions, in this sense, as a distributed attentional ritual, extending the logic of ceremonial practice into daily movement through space. The body is guided before intention is asked to perform.

Qi gong applies the same principle directly to physiology. Systematic reviews and meta-analyses show that qi gong practice reliably reduces anxiety and depression while improving psychological well-being, with effects mediated through autonomic regulation rather than through any demonstrable violation of physiology (Oh et al., 2013, pp. 1-14). Neurophysiological reviews indicate increased parasympathetic activity, reduced cortisol, and improved stress regulation resulting from structured movement and breath (Tai et al., 2019, pp. 3-9). The ritual works because it teaches the body how to exit chronic alarm. The scaffold is somatic.

Controlled studies support this conclusion. Randomized trials of external qi therapy show measurable shifts in heart-rate variability toward parasympathetic dominance, indicating improved autonomic balance under controlled conditions (Lee et al., 2005, pp. 489-494). Acute qi gong sessions have been shown to reduce anxiety and alter autonomic markers even after a single practice (Chang et al., 2018, pp. 1-10). These effects are repeatable and lawful. Ritual engages physiology; it does not bypass it.

Embodiment research outside Eastern traditions confirms the same mechanism. Brief adoption of expansive or constricted postures can alter hormonal levels, affect, and risk tolerance through ordinary neuroendocrine pathways (Carney et al., 2010, pp. 1363-1368). Research on embodied cognition shows that posture and movement bias emotional experience and memory retrieval, demonstrating that bodily configuration feeds directly back into cognition (García, 2025). The body is not a passive vehicle for ritual; it is the primary site of instruction.

Neuroscience clarifies the underlying architecture. The mirror-neuron system demonstrates that patterned movement, whether performed or observed, is encoded in shared sensorimotor circuits that shape intention, anticipation, and social understanding (Rizzolatti & Craighero, 2004, pp. 169-192). Motor control research shows that coordinated action depends on tight coupling among cortical planning, spinal execution, and biomechanical constraint (Suchan & O'Neill, 2017, pp. 1-12). Ritual choreography exerts its influence by engaging this system, not by escaping it. Movement remains physics-bound even when its meaning feels transcendent.

Taken together, ceremonial ritual, feng shui, qi gong, and embodied cognition describe the same arc. Patterned movement through space teaches stability before it teaches intention. The body learns first, the mind follows, the observer becomes visible, and only then does the operator emerge. Ritual is not power; it is training in coherence.

Beyond that threshold, form must yield. Once stability can be maintained without choreography, ritual ceases to instruct and begins to repeat itself. The operator moves through a horizonless field without external authorization, not because ritual failed, but because it succeeded fully. Axiom III therefore does not diminish ritual by calling it scaffolding. It completes it.

At the end of this progression, ritual resolves back into the mental field where it was always heading. Crowley himself was explicit that the efficacy of ritual does not reside in consecrated objects, expensive vestments, or elaborate temples, but in the operator's capacity to establish and maintain a coherent inner working space, noting repeatedly that any object can serve a magical function if it is correctly employed by the mind (Crowley, 1929/1997, pp. 92-96). A robe, a wand, or a temple matters only insofar as it assists concentration, and when concentration is stable, their material form becomes irrelevant. This is the point at which the observer is no longer distracted by externals and the entire operation relocates into what Crowley called the magician's "circle" of awareness, an interior arena where symbols, intentions, and images can be manipulated without confusion. Ritual thus translates from choreography in physical space into disciplined play within the psyche, where the observer remains distinct from the contents of the operation. The internal temple is not a metaphor but the completion of ritual's function: a stabilized mental field in which form is optional, attention is sovereign, and the operator can work without mistaking the scaffolding for the source.

Axiom IV – Symbols Are the Language of the Subconscious

This axiom rests on a constraint that cannot be bypassed by intelligence, sincerity, or discipline: the conscious mind does not directly command behavior. It explains, evaluates, and narrates, but the forces that determine salience, threat, desire, and meaning operate largely outside linear language. These deeper strata of the psyche do not respond to propositions or arguments. They respond to image, pattern, rhythm, affect, and symbolic association. Any system that seeks to influence will must therefore speak the language the psyche already uses.

Symbols are that language. A symbol compresses meaning into a form that can be apprehended all at once rather than processed sequentially. It carries emotional tone, bodily posture, memory, and implication simultaneously, bypassing debate and explanation. This is why symbols work even when belief is suspended, and why rational disagreement does not neutralize their effects. The psyche does not ask whether a symbol is true; it registers whether it is alive.

Carl Jung articulated this with unusual precision through his study of alchemy. In *Alchemical Studies*, Jung shows that medieval alchemists were not primarily engaged in proto-chemistry, nor were they merely projecting fantasies onto matter. They were working with symbols that arose spontaneously from the unconscious and were then enacted through disciplined imagination, ritualized operations, and sustained attention (Jung, 1967/1970). The alchemical texts functioned as symbolic grammars through which unconscious material could be encountered, differentiated, and transformed without overwhelming the ego. What changed was not lead into gold, but the psychic structure of the operator.

Jung was explicit that the alchemist's furnace, vessels, and substances corresponded to inner processes rather than to literal transformations of matter. The nigredo, albedo, and rubedo were not chemical stages but experiential ones, describing phases of disorientation, clarification, and integration that unfolded within the psyche when unconscious contents were engaged consciously. The symbols did not represent these processes after the fact; they *made* them possible by giving form to what would otherwise remain chaotic and inexpressible. Symbol, in this sense, is not decoration. It is containment.

This is the crucial point. The unconscious does not tolerate direct confrontation without structure. When unconscious material floods awareness without symbolic mediation, it appears as anxiety, obsession, inflation, or breakdown. Alchemy survived for centuries because it provided a symbolic operating system that allowed practitioners to work with these forces indirectly, through image and ritual, rather than through brute introspection. Jung emphasized repeatedly that the alchemical symbol stands between the ego and the unconscious as a regulating third term, preventing collapse into identification or repression.

Crowley understood this operationally, even when his language drifted. His insistence that any object could function as a magical implement if correctly associated was a recognition that the symbol's efficacy lies in mental linkage rather than material pedigree (Crowley, 1929/1997). A thimble can be a cup, a bathrobe a robe of office, because the object serves as a carrier for symbolic association within the psyche. The external form matters only insofar as it stabilizes inner attention. When that stabilization is achieved, the material form becomes optional.

This is why symbols are powerful and dangerous in equal measure. When treated as language, they translate intention into a form the psyche can act upon without confusion. When treated as reality, they invite identification. The practitioner ceases to *use* the symbol and begins to *be* it. Jung identified this as inflation: the ego's identification with archetypal contents, experienced subjectively as insight, power, or destiny (Jung, 1967/1970). Inflation is not delusion in the ordinary sense; it is a structural error in which symbol collapses into identity.

Axiom IV exists to prevent that collapse. Symbols must remain legible as symbols to the observer. The observer's role is not to reject symbols, but to maintain the distinction between symbol and self. When this distinction holds, symbols function as language. When it fails, symbols issue commands. The difference is not moral; it is functional.

In this light, ritual and symbol converge into the same interior space. Axiom III stabilized the body and revealed the observer. Axiom IV structures the mental field in which the observer operates. Jung called this the *temenos*, the protected inner space where psychic work can occur without contamination or possession. Crowley called it the circle. The alchemists called it the vessel. All three name the same requirement: a bounded inner field where symbols can be engaged without being mistaken for truth.

This is the internal temple. It is not an imagined building, but a stabilized mental arena in which image, affect, and intention can be manipulated deliberately while the observer remains intact. In this space, symbols can be activated, explored, and dissolved without residue. They are spoken fluently and then released. No external authority is required, because the grammar has been internalized.

Axiom IV therefore completes the inward turn begun with ritual. Once the body no longer needs choreography and the observer is visible, symbolic work becomes an operation within consciousness itself. The magician's task is not to worship symbols, nor to escape them, but to use them as language and then fall silent. Where symbols remain transparent, transformation is possible. Where they become opaque, enclosure begins.

Axiom V – Magick Is Engineered Synchronicity, Not Force

This axiom names what magick actually does when it works, without borrowing powers it cannot justify. Magick does not move matter directly, suspend physical law, or transmit force across space and time. When it succeeds, it produces a tightening of meaningful coincidence, a convergence between inner state and outer event that feels directed without being mechanically caused. The mistake is to interpret this felt direction as evidence of force. The correct interpretation is alignment.

Carl Jung's concept of synchronicity provides the necessary corrective language. In *Synchronicity: An Acausal Connecting Principle*, Jung defines synchronicity as the simultaneous occurrence of two or more events that are meaningfully related but not causally connected (Jung, 1952/1969). These events are not random in the ordinary sense, yet they cannot be explained by chains of cause and effect. Meaning, not energy, is the connecting term. This distinction allows magick to be described rigorously without collapsing into either superstition or reductionism.

Jung is explicit that synchronicity does not violate physical law. On the contrary, it becomes visible precisely where causal explanation reaches its limit, especially at the level of rare, emotionally charged, or archetypally saturated events. Natural law, Jung insists, is statistical rather than absolute, and therefore leaves room for acausal orderings without requiring the abandonment of causality itself. Synchronicity is not anti-causal; it is non-causal. It occupies a different explanatory register.

The Jung-Pauli correspondence deepens this point. Wolfgang Pauli, working from quantum physics, and Jung, working from depth psychology, converged on a dual-aspect or neutral-monist view in which psyche and matter are complementary expressions of an underlying order. In this framework, synchronistic events arise when inner psychic configurations and outer physical events share a common ordering principle without transmitting energy between them. Pauli emphasized that such phenomena would only appear at scales where statistics break down and individual events matter, which explains both their rarity and their resistance to experimental control. This makes synchronicity structurally incompatible with magical omnipotence.

From this perspective, magick cannot be the production of synchronicity by force, because synchronicity is not something that can be pushed into existence. Jung is clear that attempts to coerce or instrumentalize synchronistic phenomena collapse into inflation, projection, or magical thinking. The psyche does not command the archetype; it participates in it. Meaningful coincidence occurs when psychic conditions are aligned in such a way that acausal order can manifest, not when the ego demands outcome.

This distinction resolves a long-standing confusion in occult practice. When ritual, symbol, and will are effective, the practitioner's inner world becomes more coherent: attention stabilizes, affect intensifies without fragmenting, and perception sharpens. This coherence alters how choices are made, how opportunities are noticed, and how risks are taken. The external world does not bend; the practitioner's interface with it does. Over time, this produces clusters of coincidence that feel improbable from inside experience and trivial from outside description. Both perceptions are accurate, because meaning is not evenly distributed across perspectives.

Jung repeatedly observed that synchronistic phenomena are most likely to occur under conditions of high affect, existential impasse, or symbolic saturation. In clinical settings, they often accompany moments when the conscious attitude can no longer solve the problem at hand and the unconscious is constellated to compensate. The famous scarab episode illustrates this precisely: the synchronistic event did not prove magical causation, but it broke a rigid rational stance and allowed psychic transformation to proceed. The coincidence mattered because of where it landed, not because it broke physics.

This has direct implications for magick. Practices that increase symbolic coherence, emotional intensity, and observational clarity create conditions under which synchronistic patterns are more likely to be noticed and integrated. They do not create the patterns themselves. Jung warns explicitly against mistaking the archetype for a causal agent, noting that archetypal equivalences are contingent, not law-governed, and cannot be summoned on demand. When the practitioner claims authorship over coincidence, inflation follows and the phenomenon collapses.

Empirical and parapsychological work aligns with this restraint. Studies that operationalize synchronicity psychologically treat it as the experience of statistically unlikely but personally meaningful coincidence, not as evidence of mind-over-matter causation. Research linking synchronicity reporting with creativity and openness suggests that certain cognitive styles are more sensitive to pattern detection and meaning integration, again without implying ontological privilege. The psyche becomes a better reader of the field, not its ruler.

This is why engineered synchronicity must be understood as upstream work. The practitioner engineers conditions, not outcomes. Attention is trained, contradiction reduced, symbol clarified, and will focused. These factors bias probability indirectly by shaping behavior, timing, and responsiveness. When synchronicity appears, it appears as correspondence rather than command. The practitioner meets it halfway.

Failure modes are predictable when this axiom is ignored. Coincidence is reinterpreted as proof of power. Meaning is taken as causation. The observer collapses into the narrative, and discrimination is lost. Jung describes this precisely as archetypal inflation, where the ego identifies with the ordering principle rather than relating to it. At that point, synchronicity no longer guides; it misleads.

Axiom V therefore preserves magick by limiting it. Magick is the disciplined cultivation of conditions under which meaningful coincidence can emerge, be recognized, and be integrated. It is not the ability to force events, but the capacity to participate consciously in acausal order without claiming ownership of it. Synchronicity is not commanded; it is encountered.

In this sense, magick is neither illusion nor miracle. It is a practice of alignment between psyche and world that operates within the lawful structure of reality while acknowledging that causality is not the only organizing principle. The practitioner does not make things happen. The practitioner becomes capable of meeting what happens with clarity.

Axiom VI – The Observer Is the Origin

This axiom names the condition without which every other operation in this book becomes unstable. Ritual can scaffold, symbols can translate, and synchronicity can tighten probability, but none of these functions remain intelligible unless there is an observing position that is not identical with the contents of experience. Without that position, will collapses into impulse, meaning collapses into narrative, and power collapses into compensation. The observer is not an optional refinement. It is the mechanical prerequisite for any form of disciplined engagement with consciousness.

The insight is ancient, cross-cultural, and remarkably consistent once stripped of doctrinal ornament. In Advaita Vedānta, the true Self (Ātman) is described as the sākṣī, the witness that observes the three states of waking, dreaming, and deep sleep without itself undergoing change. The body sleeps, the mind dreams, and the senses awaken, yet the continuity of knowing persists across all three states. Vedānta does not infer this witness metaphysically; it points to it phenomenologically. One knows that one slept, even though no thoughts or perceptions were present, which implies an awareness that is not reducible to mental activity (Sivananda, mid-20th century).

Crucially, Advaita insists that this witness is not a second entity hiding behind experience. It is not an inner homunculus or metaphysical observer standing apart from the world. It is consciousness itself, self-luminous and self-evident, appearing as the field in which all mental and physical phenomena arise. What changes are the contents; what does not change is the fact of awareness. The error of ordinary identification lies in mistaking transient mental states for the knower of those states.

Yogic traditions operationalize this distinction with precision. Terms such as draṣṭā (seer) and sākṣī (witness) are not speculative abstractions, but functional designations for a stance that can be trained. Through practices that emphasize observing vṛttis — thoughts, emotions, sensations — as objects rather than as self, identification gradually weakens. The practitioner learns to see anger arise without becoming angry, desire arise without becoming desire, and fear arise without collapsing into fear. This does not suppress experience; it re-locates identity (Light, 2020; Tadatmananda, 2017).

In this framework, liberation is not an ecstatic state or a metaphysical ascent, but the stabilization of sākṣī-bhāva, the stance of witnessing itself. The process and the goal coincide, because the more consistently one abides as witness, the clearer it becomes that this witnessing awareness was never absent. The world, in this view, is a modulation within consciousness, and consciousness witnesses its own display without undergoing alteration (Nikhilananda, 2009).

Buddhist philosophy approaches the same terrain through systematic negation rather than affirmation, yet arrives at a structurally identical function. Early Buddhist analysis decomposes experience into impermanent aggregates — sensation, feeling, perception, volition, and consciousness — and shows that no enduring self can be found among them. The practice of mindfulness is not aimed at discovering a hidden observer, but at observing experience so exhaustively that the assumption of an inner owner becomes untenable (SuttaCentral discussion, 2018).

Importantly, Buddhism does not deny observation; it denies *ownership*. There is seeing, knowing, and discerning, but no metaphysically privileged watcher standing apart from the flow. Contemporary

Buddhist teachers emphasize that "not-self" is a strategy rather than an ontology: a tool to dismantle clinging, not a claim about ultimate substance. The observing function remains, but it is understood as a process rather than as an entity (Ṭhānissaro Bhikkhu, 2013).

This difference between Advaita and Buddhism is often overstated. At the level of practice, both traditions converge on the same operational outcome: a loosening of identification with mental contents and a stabilization of awareness that is less reactive, less narrative-bound, and more precise. Whether one calls this awareness Ātman or simply "knowing without owner" is secondary to the functional result. The observer is revealed not as a thing, but as a capacity.

Modern psychology and neuroscience approach this same capacity through the language of metacognition. Metacognitive reflection is defined as the ability to monitor and regulate one's own cognitive and emotional processes, effectively creating a buffer between impulse and action (Varpio et al., 2024). This capacity allows individuals to question automatic interpretations, notice emotional bias, and revise decisions before they harden into behavior. In psychological terms, this is an "inner observer," even if no metaphysical claims are made about its ultimate nature.

Neuroscientific research maps this phenomenology onto identifiable network dynamics. The default mode network, associated with self-referential thought and narrative identity, becomes less dominant during practices that emphasize present-moment awareness. Mindfulness training, in particular, is associated with reduced activation in medial prefrontal regions linked to autobiographical self-story, alongside increased engagement of sensory and attentional networks (Farb et al., 2007). Subjectively, this shift is experienced as the difference between being lost in thought and observing thought.

Farb and colleagues explicitly describe this as the cultivation of a "witnessing self," a mode of awareness that can observe both sensory experience and narrative processes without fusing with either. They emphasize that this witnessing mode is phenomenologically distinct from both discursive self-talk and raw sensation. It is not content, but context. Again, neuroscience does not resolve metaphysics, but it confirms the functional reality of the observer as a regulatory stance.

Across all these frameworks, the same mechanical insight emerges. When the observer is absent or collapsed into thought, will becomes contaminated. Action is driven by fear, compensation, or unconscious pattern, even when dressed in spiritual language. This is why systems that emphasize power, ritual, or identity without stabilizing the observer reliably devolve into enclosure. Control replaces contact. Intensity replaces clarity.

When the observer is present, something different becomes possible. Symbols remain symbols. Ritual becomes optional rather than compulsory. Synchronicity can be recognized without inflation. The practitioner can engage meaning without mistaking meaning for authorship. This is the point at which magick ceases to be performative and becomes precise.

This axiom is therefore called origin not because the observer is a metaphysical first cause, but because it is the point from which all other operations become honest. It is the only stance from which one can tell the difference between alignment and delusion, between probability and fantasy, between participation and control. Every tradition that matures eventually circles back to this recognition, not out of mysticism, but out of necessity.

Without the observer, there is no discipline. With it, there is no need for belief.

Axiom VII – Unbroken Observation Is the Impossible Requirement

This axiom states the final constraint, and it is the one that makes all other axioms non-negotiable. If ritual is scaffolding, if symbols are a language, if magick operates through meaningful coincidence rather than force, and if the observer is the origin of any honest operation, then one requirement remains absolute. The observer must remain present without interruption, not intermittently, not only in formal practice, but continuously across affect, circumstance, and time. This is not an aspirational flourish or a mystical exaggeration. It is a mechanical demand implied by every system that takes consciousness seriously.

Classical yoga opens with this admission rather than hiding it. Patañjali defines yoga as the restraint or cessation of the mind's fluctuations, yogaḥ citta-vṛtti-nirodhaḥ, which immediately implies that fluctuation is the baseline condition of ordinary consciousness (Patañjali, Yoga Sūtra I.2; YogaRenew, 2025). The mind is not described as occasionally distracted but as continuously modified by perception, delusion, imagination, sleep, and memory, with practice defined as repeatedly bringing it back from whatever it is doing. Even the grammar of the sutra is a diagnostic statement before it becomes an instruction. In effect, the tradition begins by saying that unbroken observation is not the human default but the human problem.

Patañjali then makes the mechanism explicit in a way that anticipates modern attention science. The restraint of vṛttis, he says, is achieved through abhyāsa and vairāgya, persistent practice and non-attachment, a formulation that only makes sense if the mind reliably slips back into motion (Patañjali, Yoga Sūtra I.12; Yoga Journal, 2017). Abhyāsa is not a sudden insight but a long-term training arc, and vairāgya is not indifference but the repeated refusal to fuse with what arises. The sutras do not pretend that once the observer is seen, the observer stays. They treat relapse into distraction as normal and re-centering as the work.

The Bhagavad Gītā goes further by letting the exemplary disciple say what everyone experiences. Arjuna, who is neither weak nor unserious, tells Kṛṣṇa that the mind is restless, turbulent, strong, and obstinate, and he considers it as difficult to control as the wind (Bhagavad Gītā 6.34; Bhagavad Gita for All, n.d.). That line is often read devotionally, but its practical meaning is blunt. If even a disciplined warrior-mind cannot hold attention steady, the problem is not motivation. The problem is architecture.

Later teachers intensify the metaphor precisely because the experience is universal. Vivekananda's "maddened monkey" parable portrays the mind as naturally restless, then made worse by desire, jealousy, and pride, explicitly concluding that control is extraordinarily difficult (Vivekananda, 1896; as paraphrased in Gidwani, 2014). Sivananda uses similar language, describing the mind as wandering, variety-seeking, discontinuous, and jumpy, emphasizing that steadiness is not a trait but a discipline (Sivananda, 2025). These are not rhetorical insults aimed at the practitioner. They are a refusal to romanticize the human cognitive baseline.

Advaita literature acknowledges the same constraint even while affirming the witness as ever-present. The witness may be timeless, but the mind's tendency is to stray, and therefore the practical instruction is not to "arrive" at the Self once, but to return again and again whenever attention disperses. The Ramana tradition is unusually clear here, presenting wandering as the mind's natural tendency and framing progress as the shortening of intervals between returns until wandering loses momentum (Ramana Maharshi, as summarized in r/AdvaitaVedanta, 2025). In this framing, the issue is not that the witness disappears, but that energy leaks through scattered thought, and the practitioner repeatedly reclaims it by fixing attention again. Unbroken observation is not denied; it is treated as the far end of training, not the beginning.

Classical Advaita also makes the end-point severity unmistakable. Śaṅkara's language about manonāśa, the dissolution of mind as mind, is not a casual poeticism but a description of how total the requirement becomes if duality is to disappear (Śaṅkara on Gauḍapāda's Māṇḍūkya Kārikā III.31; summarized in Das, 2022). Whether one takes that as metaphysical, phenomenological, or pedagogical, the practical implication is consistent with Yoga Sūtra I.2 and Gītā 6.34. The stable, uninterrupted observer-position is not a gentle habit layered onto ordinary cognition. It is a radical stabilization that ordinary cognition resists.

This is where Book Three's claim becomes precise. The observer is easy to recognize and nearly impossible to sustain. Recognition is a moment; sustainability is a life. The gap between those two explains why so many systems produce brief gains followed by enclosure, myth inflation, or collapse into ritual dependency. When observation breaks, the system fills the break with explanations, and those explanations become identity.

Contemporary cognitive science reaches the same conclusion using different instruments and less metaphysical language. Sustained attention tasks show a vigilance decrement even over brief periods, with performance declining as time-on-task increases and mind wandering rising alongside it (Schwartzman et al., 2025). This is not a failure of character, because the decrement appears reliably even when participants are motivated and instructed to remain focused. Reviews of vigilance across applied domains such as monitoring and screening conclude that this decline is a general limitation of the sustained attention system rather than a rare malfunction (Warm et al., 2019). The nervous system simply does not maintain steady high-fidelity attention indefinitely.

Objective physiological markers show that fluctuation is not merely subjective reporting. Measures such as reaction-time variability and related indicators move between "in-the-zone" and "out-of-the-zone" states even when participants intend to remain stable, indicating that attention oscillates independently of will (Chidharom et al., 2024). This aligns with the contemplative claim that the observer-position is not maintained by effort alone because effort itself is content, and content fluctuates. The mind does not drift occasionally; it drifts structurally. What is being trained in practice is not the elimination of drift but the speed and cleanliness of return.

Large-scale experience sampling makes the same point in everyday life. People spend a substantial portion of waking time in stimulus-independent thought, and this mind-wandering baseline is associated with self-referential network activity, which is why contemplative training is better described as managing default tendencies than abolishing them (Killingsworth & Gilbert, 2010). Even in experienced meditators, default-mode patterns are attenuated and better regulated, not eradicated, supporting the claim that the best practitioners do not become permanently drift-free so much as faster at re-stabilizing (Brewer et al., 2011). This matters because it removes the fantasy that unbroken observation is simply a matter of wanting it enough. It is a neurological demand that exceeds ordinary capacity.

Working memory imposes a second hard limit on what continuous observation could even mean. Even in ideal conditions, the central store that supports deliberate monitoring is limited to a small number of meaningful units, often estimated around three to five "chunks," which constrains how much can be held in reflective awareness at once (Cowan, 2010). Subjective experience may feel continuous and rich, but the monitoring bandwidth is narrow. This makes the fantasy of "always observing everything" biologically incoherent. The actual task is

114

narrower and harsher: to keep the observer-position intact while content changes, not to track every content in detail.

Temporal bottlenecks add a third constraint that traditions intuited as the impossibility of continuous precision. The attentional blink shows that when targets arrive in rapid succession, awareness often fails to fully process the second within a short window, revealing a processing bottleneck even in brief time frames (Martens & Marois, 2011). Recent work that decomposes attentional blink effects into subcomponents shows selective impairment of sensitivity, reinforcing that attention cannot be fully engaged continuously at high resolution (Halder et al., 2025). Even before we reach mystical claims, the machinery fails on millisecond scales. This is what "unbroken" is up against.

Metacognitive monitoring, the psychological analogue of the witness-function, also degrades under load. When attention is divided between tasks, metacognitive control suffers more than monitoring, indicating that the very capacity to regulate one's own cognition is resource-dependent and fragile (Schneider & Kray, 2021). This is exactly what practitioners report in the language of vṛtti, kleśa, and saṃskāra: the observer is easiest to maintain in stillness and hardest to maintain in emotional traffic. The tradition's insistence on long training is not spiritual elitism; it is an accurate description of limited resources. The observer-function costs something, and under pressure the system spends it.

This is why Axiom VII must be stated plainly. Real magick, understood as disciplined probability alignment under the constraints of physics, requires a degree of coherence that cannot be sustained by ordinary humans for long. Unbroken observation is the condition under which intention would remain clean, symbol would remain transparent, and synchronicity could be met without inflation, but that condition is neurologically and psychologically extreme. Most practitioners therefore experience it in fragments, and the fragments are enough to

115

seduce them into over-claiming. The axiom exists to prevent that seduction from becoming a doctrine.

The final implication is sobering and clarifying. The rarity of stable magical effects is not primarily a failure of method, tradition, or ritual technology. It is a predictable consequence of attentional drift, working-memory limits, temporal bottlenecks, and the mind's innate tendency to re-identify with content. Traditions knew this long before labs measured it, which is why they framed the mind as wind-like, monkey-like, and naturally wandering, and why they prescribed return rather than conquest. The impossible requirement does not negate practice; it defines it.

When this axiom is respected, the practitioner stops demanding permanence and begins valuing fidelity. The measure becomes not whether one can remain unbroken, but how quickly one can notice the break, return without shame, and continue without inflation. That is what remains human, honest, and workable. Unbroken observation is the impossible requirement, and acknowledging that impossibility is the final discipline that keeps all the other axioms clean.

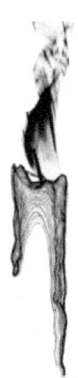

Closure

Integration is not reconciliation with what was rejected, nor a return to comfort, nor a correction of excess. It is the capacity to remain intact while being altered, to allow experience to register without surrendering authorship, and to revise orientation without collapsing into submission or freezing into defense. Rupture was necessary wherever guilt, coercion, or imposed meaning distorted agency, and its tools remain valid wherever those conditions persist. But a self that cannot move beyond rupture remains bound to the moment of its escape, refining defenses long after the threat has passed. What determines whether liberation becomes evolution or enclosure is not belief, identity, or intensity, but structural capacity: permeability without collapse, will without compulsion, power without rigidity. At that threshold, no system can proceed on your behalf. The work is no longer to break free, but to live without the need to keep breaking.

BOOK ONE — REFERENCES

Arweck, E., & Clarke, P. B. (Eds.). (1997). *New religious movements in Western Europe*. Routledge.

Barker, E. (1984). *The making of a Moonie: Brainwashing or choice?* Blackwell.

Bauman, Z. (2000). *Liquid modernity*. Polity Press.

Beckford, J. A. (1985). *Cult controversies: The societal response to new religious movements*. Tavistock.

Black, R. (2011). *Identity transitions and the project of the self: A study of former members of world-rejecting new religious movements* (Doctoral dissertation). University of Newcastle.

Carrette, J. R., & King, R. (2005). *Selling spirituality: The silent takeover of religion*. Routledge.

Dyrendal, A., Lewis, J. R., & Petersen, J. A. (2015). *The invention of Satanism*. Oxford University Press.

Erikson, E. H. (1968). *Identity: Youth and crisis*. W. W. Norton.

Farias, M., & Wikholm, C. (2015). *The Buddha pill: Can meditation change you?* Watkins.

Hanegraaff, W. J. (1996). *New Age religion and Western culture*. Brill.

Hassan, S. (1990). *Combating cult mind control*. Park Street Press.

Heelas, P. (1996). *The New Age movement: The celebration of the self and the sacralization of modernity*. Blackwell.

Horkheimer, M., & Adorno, T. W. (2002). *Dialectic of enlightenment*. Stanford University Press.

Houtman, D., & Aupers, S. (2007). The spiritual turn and the decline of tradition. *Journal for the Scientific Study of Religion, 46*(3), 305-320.

Introvigne, M. (2016). *Satanism: A social history*. Brill.

Krishnan, V. (2022). Relationship between Vedic personality traits and stress. *Indian Journal of Psychiatry, 64*(4), 356-364.

Lavey, A. S. (1969). *The Satanic Bible*. Avon Books.

Laycock, J. P. (2015). Atheistic Satanism: The Church of Satan, rebellion, and the construction of the self. *Nova Religio, 19*(1), 49-64.

Lewis, J. R. (2001). *The Church of Satan: A history of the world's most notorious religion*. Oxford University Press.

Lewis, J. R. (2012). Diabolical authority: Anton *Lavey* and the Church of Satan. In *The Cambridge companion to new religious movements* (pp. 99-117). Cambridge University Press.

Petersen, J. A. (2008). Modern Satanism as an example of secular religion. *Numen, 55*(4), 409-433.

Puligandla, R. (1975). *Fundamentals of Indian philosophy*. Abingdon Press.

Redbeard, R. (1896). *Might is right*. Author.

Ritzer, G. (1993). *The McDonaldization of society*. Pine Forge Press.

Sprankle, E., et al. (2019). Satanist identity, stigma, and mental health. *International Journal for the Study of New Religions, 10*(2), 163-185.

Stausberg, M., & Engler, S. (Eds.). (2011). *The Routledge handbook of research methods in the study of religion*. Routledge.

Streib, H., & Hood, R. W. (2013). Understanding religious conversion and deconversion. In *The Oxford handbook of the psychology of religion and spirituality* (pp. 201-222). Oxford University Press.

Wolf, D. (1999). A psychometric analysis of the three gunas. *Psychological Reports, 84*(3), 1379-1390.

BOOK TWO — REFERENCES

Barrett, L. F., & Simmons, W. K. (2015). Interoceptive predictions in the brain. *Nature Reviews Neuroscience, 16*(7), 419-429. https://doi.org/10.1038/nrn3950

Berkman, E. T., Livingston, J. L., & Kahn, L. E. (2017). Finding the self in self-regulation: The identity-value model. *Psychological Inquiry, 28*(2-3), 77-98.

Bhakti Niskama Shanta, B. N. (2015). Life and consciousness: The Vedāntic view. *Communicative & Integrative Biology, 8*(5), e1085138.

Bhargav, H., et al. (2023). Composition of yoga-philosophy-based mental traits (gunas) in major psychiatric disorders: A trans-diagnostic approach. *Frontiers in Psychology, 14*, 1075060.

Blackburn, S. (1993). *Essays in quasi-realism.* Oxford University Press.

Borghi, A. M., et al. (2017). The challenge of abstract concepts. *Psychological Bulletin, 143*(3), 263-292.

Brooks, D. R. (1990). *The secret of the three cities: An introduction to Hindu Śākta tantrism.* University of Chicago Press.

Chandler, M. J., Boyes, M., & Ball, L. (1983). Relativism and stages of reflective judgment. *Human Development, 26*(4), 210-224.

Costin, V., & Vignoles, V. L. (2020). Meaning, nihilism, and well-being. *Journal of Personality and Social Psychology, 118*(2), 234-259.

Craig, A. D. (2009). How do you feel—now? The anterior insula and human awareness. *Nature Reviews Neuroscience, 10*(1), 59-70.

Csordas, T. J. (1994). *The sacred self: A cultural phenomenology of charismatic healing*. University of California Press.

Damasio, A. R. (1994). *Descartes' error: Emotion, reason, and the human brain*. Putnam.

Davidson, D. (1963). Actions, reasons, and causes. *The Journal of Philosophy, 60*(23), 685-700.

Dehaene, S., Lau, H., & Kouider, S. (2024). What is consciousness, and could machines have it? *Science, 358*(6362), 486-492.

Do, A. T., Wahlen, S., & Chazal, A. (2021). Recurrent neural networks. *arXiv*. https://arxiv.org/abs/2101.02524

Erikson, E. H. (1950). *Childhood and society*. W. W. Norton.

Farb, N. A. S., Segal, Z. V., & Anderson, A. K. (2015). Mindfulness meditation training alters cortical representations of interoceptive attention. *Social Cognitive and Affective Neuroscience, 8*(1), 15-26.

Furnham, A., & Marks, J. (2013). Tolerance of ambiguity: A review of the concept, its measurement, and applications. *Current Psychology, 32*(3), 232-248.

Gibbard, A. (2003). *Thinking how to live*. Harvard University Press.

Haidt, J. (2001). The emotional dog and its rational tail. *Psychological Review, 108*(4), 814-834.

Haidt, J., & Bjorklund, F. (2008). Social intuitionists answer six questions about moral psychology. In W. Sinnott-Armstrong (Ed.), *Moral psychology* (Vol. 2, pp. 181-217). MIT Press.

Hareesh. (2016). *The real story on the chakras.* https://hareesh.org/blog/2016/2/5/the-real-story-on-the-chakras

Hartmann, E. (1991). *Boundaries in the mind: A new psychology of personality.* Basic Books.

Kegan, R. (1982). *The evolving self: Problem and process in human development.* Harvard University Press.

Khalsa, S. S., et al. (2018). Interoception and mental health: A roadmap. *Biological Psychiatry: Cognitive Neuroscience and Neuroimaging, 3*(6), 501-513.

Mallinson, J., & Singleton, M. (2017). *Roots of yoga.* Penguin Classics.

Maslow, A. H. (1943). A theory of human motivation. *Psychological Review, 50*(4), 370-396.

Oyserman, D. (2010). Identity-based motivation. *The Counseling Psychologist, 38*(7), 1001-1043.

Papus. (2009). *The Tarot of the Bohemians.* (Original work published 1892)

Porges, S. W. (2011). *The polyvagal theory.* W. W. Norton.

Pulvermüller, F. (2013). How neurons make meaning. *Trends in Cognitive Sciences, 17*(9), 458-470.

Scanlon, T. M. (1998). *What we owe to each other.* Harvard University Press.

Sartre, J.-P. (1956). *Being and nothingness* (H. Barnes, Trans.). Washington Square Press. (Original work published 1943)

Seth, A. K. (2013). Interoceptive inference. *Trends in Cognitive Sciences, 17*(11), 565-573.

Stanford Encyclopedia of Philosophy. (2018). *Consciousness*. Stanford
University. https://plato.stanford.edu/entries/consciousness/

Tajfel, H., & Turner, J. C. (1979). Intergroup conflict theory. In W. G.
Austin & S. Worchel (Eds.), *The social psychology of intergroup relations* (pp.
33-47). Brooks/Cole.

Yalom, I. D. (1980). *Existential psychotherapy*. Basic Books.

Jung, C. G. (2009). *The Red Book: Liber Novus*. W. W. Norton &
Company.

BOOK THREE — REFERENCES

Bhagavad Gita for All. (n.d.). *Bhagavad Gītā 6.34*.
https://www.bhagavadgitaforall.com/verses/6-34

Bialy, S., & Loeb, A. (2019). On the anomalous acceleration of 1I/2017
U1 'Oumuamua. *The Astrophysical Journal Letters, 876*(1), L26.
https://ui.adsabs.harvard.edu/abs/2019ApJ...876L..26S/abstract

Bhikkhu, T. (2013). *Selves & not-self: The Buddhist teaching on anattā*. Access
to Insight.

Brewer, J. A., et al. (2011). Meditation experience is associated with
differences in default mode network activity and connectivity.
Proceedings of the National Academy of Sciences, 108(50), 20254-20259.

Bruun, O. (2003). *Fengshui in China: Geomantic divination between state
orthodoxy and popular religion*. University of Hawai'i Press.

Bruun, O., & Yang, F. (Eds.). (2011). *Fengshui: Imagining place in a placed world*. Brill.

Cambray, J. (2021). *Synchronicity: An acausal connecting principle*. International Association for Analytical Psychology.

Carney, D. R., et al. (2010). Power posing: Brief nonverbal displays affect neuroendocrine levels and risk tolerance. *Psychological Science, 21*(10), 1363-1368.

Chang, H.-H., et al. (2018). Acute effects of qigong exercise on meridian electrical conductance and autonomic nervous system balance in older practitioners. *Aging and Disease, 9*(1), 1-10.

Chidharom, N., et al. (2024). Objective markers of sustained attention fluctuate independently of subjective experience. *bioRxiv*.

Cowan, N. (2010). The magical mystery four: How is working memory capacity limited, and why? *Current Directions in Psychological Science, 19*(1), 51-57.

Crowley, A. (1997). *Magick in theory and practice*. Castle Books. (Original work published 1929)

Das, T. (2022, March 17). *Advaita Vedanta - all thoughts must go! (Manonasa)*. https://tomdas.com/2022/03/18/advaita-vedanta-all-thoughts-must-go-the-need-to-still-the-mind-and-end-all-thinking-according-to-shankara/

Farb, N. A. S., et al. (2007). Attending to the present: Mindfulness meditation reveals distinct neural modes of self-reference. *Social Cognitive and Affective Neuroscience, 2*(4), 313-322.

Garisto, D. (2018, December 1). Spooky quantum action passes the ultimate test. *Scientific American.*

Gidwani, C. (2014, July 5). Human mind is like a monkey... Swami Vivekananda.

Halder, T. K. M., et al. (2025). Distinct neural bases of subcomponents of the attentional blink. *eLife, 14,* e97098.

Jung, C. G. (1969). *Synchronicity: An acausal connecting principle* (R. F. C. Hull, Trans.). Princeton University Press.

Jung, C. G. (1970). *Alchemical studies* (R. F. C. Hull, Trans.). Princeton University Press.

Kaplan, S. (1995). The restorative benefits of nature: Toward an integrative framework. *Journal of Environmental Psychology, 15*(3), 169-182.

Killingsworth, M. A., & Gilbert, D. T. (2010). A wandering mind is an unhappy mind. *Science, 330*(6006), 932.

Kripal, J. J. (2010). *Authors of the impossible: The paranormal and the sacred.* University of Chicago Press.

Lee, H., et al. (2005). Effects of qi-therapy (external qigong) on cardiac autonomic tone. *Journal of Alternative and Complementary Medicine, 11*(3), 489-494.

Light, E. (2020). *Antar mouna.* Emily Light Yoga.

Main, R. (2018). Research on synchronicity: Status and prospects. *Journal of Analytical Psychology, 63*(4), 535-554.

Mak, M. Y., & So, A. T. P. (2010). Scientific feng shui for the built environment. *International Journal of Architectural Research, 4*(2-3), 310-323.

Mansfield, V. (1998). Synchronicity, causality, and acausality. *Journal of the American Institute for Parapsychology, 42*, 145-166.

Martens, J. B., & Marois, R. (2011). Unmasking the attentional blink. *Journal of Experimental Psychology: Human Perception and Performance, 37*(3), 792-807.

Moskowitz, C. (2025, March 19). Shocking dark energy findings challenge the standard model of cosmology. *Scientific American*.

Nádai, L., Varlaki, P., & Bokor, J. (2009). Jung-Pauli theory and the concept of synchronicity. In *Proceedings of the Pauli Conference*. Óbuda University.

Nikhilananda, S. (2009). The witnessing mind. *Life Positive*.

Oh, S.-H., et al. (2013). The effects of qigong on anxiety, depression, and psychological well-being. *Frontiers in Psychiatry, 4*, Article 91.

Papus. (2009). *The Tarot of the Bohemians*. (Original work published 1892)

Pauli, W. (1994). *Atom and archetype: The Pauli/Jung letters, 1932-1958*. Princeton University Press.

Schneider, G. A. K., & Kray, J. (2021). Dividing attention impairs metacognitive control more than monitoring. *Psychonomic Bulletin & Review, 28*(4), 1270-1281.

Sivananda, S. (n.d.). Atman is witness of three states. In *Self-Knowledge*. Divine Life Society.

Strickland, A. (2025, January 24). Two mysterious fast radio bursts originated from wildly different places in space. *CNN*.

SuttaCentral Discussion Forum. (2018). How do you directly observe anattā?

Tai, K. S., et al. (2019). The neurophysiological and psychological mechanisms of qigong for depression. *Frontiers in Psychiatry*, 10, Article 820.

Tadatmananda, S. (2017). *Sakshi - The awareful witness*. Arsha Bodha Center.

Thalbourne, M. A. (1996). Synchronicity, an acausal connecting principle. *British Journal of Psychology*, 87(3), 389-399.

Varpio, A., et al. (2024). Metacognition: An overview. *Perspectives on Medical Education*, 13, Article 5.

Vernon, D., & Thalbourne, M. A. (2002). A principal components analysis of a measure of belief in synchronicity. *Journal of Parapsychology*, 66, 37-55.

Walach, H., & Stillfried, N. (2011). Generalized entanglement: A new theoretical model. *Journal of Alternative and Complementary Medicine*, 17(